THE
ARTS & CRAFTS
HOUSE

THE ARTS & CRAFTS HOUSE

ADRIAN TINNISWOOD

MITCHELL BEAZLEY

The Arts & Crafts House
Adrian Tinniswood

First published in Great Britain in 1999 by Mitchell Beazley,
an imprint of Octopus Publishing Group Ltd,
2–4 Heron Quays, London, E14 4JP

Executive Editor **Alison Starling**
Executive Art Editor **Vivienne Brar**
Project Editor **Elisabeth Faber**
Designer **Martin Lovelock**
Picture Research **Jenny Faithfull**, **Claire Gouldstone**
Production **Rachel Staveley**
Index **Ann Barratt**

ISBN 1 84000 062 7

A CIP record for this book is available from the
British Library

Set in Centaur MT

Printed and bound in China by Toppan Printing Co.,
(HK) Ltd.

CONTENTS

Introduction: Designs for Living   6

MORRIS & CO.   10
Red House   Philip Webb   14
The Firm   The work of Morris & Co.   18
Cragside   Richard Norman Shaw   22
Anti-scrape   The Society for the Protection
   of Ancient Buildings   24
Wightwick Manor   Edward Ould   26
Standen   Philip Webb   30
Melsetter House   W. R. Lethaby   34

THE ARCHITECT AT HOME   38
Bloemenwerf   Henry van de Velde   42
Ragdale   Howard Van Doren Shaw   46
Das englische Haus   Hermann Muthesius   50
Haus Olbrich   Joseph Maria Olbrich   52
Hvitträsk   Herman Gesellius, Armas Lindgren,
   and Eliel Saarinen   56
A Place in the Country   60
Hilles   Detmar Blow   62
Owlpen Manor   Norman Jewson   66

AMERICA THE BEAUTIFUL   70
Grayoaks   Bernard Maybeck   74
Gustav Stickley   Founder of the Craftsman Workshops   78
The Gamble House   Charles and Henry Greene   82
How the West Was Won   86
Hollyhock House   Frank Lloyd Wright   88
Casa del Herrero   George Washington Smith   92
The Gillette Ranch   Wallace Neff   96
The Williams House   Julia Morgan   100

COUNTRY LIFE   104
Over the Rainbow   Country Life magazine   108
Munstead Wood   Edwin Lutyens   110
The Arts & Crafts Garden   114
Broadleys   C. F. A. Voysey   118
Stoneywell Cottage   Ernest Gimson   122
Eden in Suburbia   Urban development   126
Home Place   Edward Schroeder Prior   130
No Magic Quality   Ambrose Heal and the
   commercialization of craft   134
Rodmarton Manor   Ernest Barnsley   136

AN INTERNATIONAL STYLE   140
The Glessner House   Henry Hobson Richardson   144
International Exhibitions   How the Arts and Crafts
   movement was spread abroad   148
Hill House   Charles Rennie Mackintosh   150
The Art Nouveau Movement   154
Laverockdale   Robert Stodart Lorimer   158
The Storer House   Frank Lloyd Wright   162
The End of the Movement   166

Bibliography   170
Index   171
Acknowledgments   176

DESIGNS FOR LIVING

The origins of a movement

The Arts and Crafts movement acquired its name in 1888, when the first exhibition of the newly formed Arts and Crafts Exhibition Society opened at the New Gallery in London and, according to a visitor, "a thrill of pleasure and surprise ran through the spectators" at the sight of William Morris's tapestries, William de Morgan's tiles, Walter Crane's wallpapers, and Edward Burne-Jones's designs for stained glass.

But the union of Arts and Crafts was born out of reaction, and its roots go back to 1851 and the "Great Exhibition of the Works of Industry of All Nations," when over 144 days, six million visitors thronged Joseph Paxton's eighteen-acre Crystal Palace to stare at mock-medieval chalices, slabs of glass made to imitate marble, and a Town Mansion House for bees. They saw steam engines plastered with Gothic, Greek, and Egyptian architectural ornament; a bed that collapsed each morning and catapulted its occupant to his or her feet; and a doctor's walking stick that concealed an enema. Queen Victoria, who opened the Great Exhibition as massed choirs sang the Hallelujah Chorus, was delighted: "Our people have shown such taste in their manufactures," she said. More discriminating visitors disagreed, seeing the cheap, mass-produced household goods and incongruous "art-objects" as a dreadful indictment of the state of British design; a young William Morris dismissed the exhibits as "wonderfully ugly." If this was the best the most advanced industrial society in the world could do, then perhaps it was time to learn from the past and get back to pre-industrial basics.

LEFT **The Arts and Crafts movement was above all an act of rebellion – rebellion against a complacent middle class that could cheerfully ignore the appalling consequences that industrialization and factory labour had for the poorer members of society.**

RIGHT **Intended as a shop window for British industry, the Great Exhibition, held in 1851 at the Crystal Palace in London, attracted large numbers of visitors. To Morris and his followers, however, the items on display exemplified the way in which mass-production had dehumanized the worker, who was denied any meaningful part in the creative process.**

LEFT The Morris and Burne-Jones families, photographed in 1874 in the garden of The Grange, the Burne-Joneses' home in Fulham, London. From left to right: Margaret, Edward, Philip, and Georgiana Burne-Jones, and May, William, Jane, and Jenny Morris.

The drive to reunite artist and craftsman that resulted from the shocked reaction to the Great Exhibition became a moral crusade. In its emphasis on high standards, honest construction, and the social benefits of good design to both producer and consumer, it was destined to change the western world. By the early 1900s, there were few places in northern Europe or the United States that remained untouched by the eloquence of its arguments, of which the Arts and Crafts house was the supreme embodiment.

All the same, the movement was doomed from the start. It deluded itself by believing that society could turn back the clock to before the Industrial Revolution. It was hypocritical and elitist, in that it pretended to serve the needs of working people, while only the rich could afford its expensive, handmade products. And it sought refuge in a misty past, instead of embracing the future.

Yet even today, seventy years after the Arts and Crafts movement gave up the fight against the industrial age and descended into the quaint and banal, only the hardest of hearts can look on a Morris chair and not be moved by its beauty, or walk around a Greene & Greene bungalow, and not feel the fire that burned. The movement's heroes must have been doing something right. And that is what this book is about.

ABOVE A high-Victorian design for a window treatment, seen in an illustration from *Cassell's Household Guide* (1869–71). The simple styles favoured by Arts and Crafts designers were a direct response to overblown furnishings such as these.

RIGHT The north front of Kelmscott Manor, the Elizabethan farmhouse beside the Thames in Oxfordshire, leased by William Morris as a summer retreat in 1871 and described by him as "the loveliest haunt of ancient peace that can well be imagined."

MORRIS & CO.

Ruskin, Morris, and the birth of Arts and Crafts

The history of the Arts and Crafts house begins with two lunatics. One was Augustus Welby Pugin (1812–52), the fanatical prophet of the Gothic Revival, whose prophecies of "fitness for purpose" showed the way to a revolution in architectural theory, and whose fanaticism finally toppled over into insanity. The other was John Ruskin (1819–1900), whose fame rests on the parallels he drew between morality and architecture and his argument that the Industrial Revolution had dehumanized the artisan, turning him into a machine, robbing him of his creativity, and leading to buildings, artefacts, and decorative objects that were ugly because they had no soul. (Ruskin will also always be remembered for his failure to consummate his marriage after he discovered, to his horror, that his teenage bride had pubic hair.) His own gradual descent into madness, which came at the end of a long career as one of Victorian England's most challenging thinkers, was less dramatic than that of Pugin, but so much more poignant.

But if the Arts and Crafts house had unstable grandparents, its father was eminently sane. Nevertheless, William Morris (1834–96), the founder and figurehead of the movement, raged against the age with a passion that made Ruskin seem positively effete. As a young student at Oxford in 1853, Morris had read Ruskin's scathing condemnation of contemporary design in *The Stones of Venice*, a revisionist survey of Venetian architecture from the Byzantine period to the eighteenth century. Ruskin argued that the Gothic had marked a high point in the history of Venice, that the Renaissance was a regrettable lapse, and that the rise and fall of the Venetian builder's art depended on the moral or immoral "temper of the State." The superiority of the Gothic lay not only in its aesthetic appeal, but in the fact that it expressed a creative – and therefore morally valid – relationship between the mason as craftsman and the work he produced. Moreover,

Ruskin went on to draw parallels with contemporary society, setting himself firmly against the spirit of the age and berating his readers for their confident and complacent belief in progress and the benefits of industrialization:

And now, reader, look round this English room of yours, about which you have been proud so often, because the work of it was so good and strong, and the ornaments of it so finished. Examine again all those accurate mouldings, and perfect polishings, and unerring adjustments of the seasoned wood and tempered steel. Many a time you have exulted over them, and thought how great England was, because her slightest work was done so thoroughly. Alas! if read rightly, these perfectnesses are signs of a slavery in our England a thousand times more bitter and more degrading than that of the scourged African, or helot Greek.

Morris later wrote that "The Nature of Gothic," the chapter in *The Stones of Venice* from which this passage comes, "seemed to point out a new road on which the world should travel." It certainly led him – and us – along a new road. It led him to embark on a crusade to improve architecture and design by uniting art and craft. It led to the formation of one of the most influential design companies Britain has ever known. And it led directly to the Arts and Crafts house.

In 1890 the society hostess Lady Mount-Temple recalled her uncomfortable encounter twenty-five years earlier with the painter Dante Gabriel Rossetti, who was then a partner in the firm of Morris, Marshall, Faulkner & Co. and a close friend of Morris:

> When we furnished our dear little house in Curzon Street, nothing would please us but watered paper on the walls, garlands of roses tied with blue bows, glazed chintzes with bunches of roses...The most lovely ornaments we had in perfect harmony, gilt pelicans or swans or candlesticks, Minton's imitation of Sèvres, and gilt bows everywhere. One day [Rossetti] was dining alone with us. I began to ask him if it were possible to suggest improvements. "Well," he said frankly, "I should begin by burning everything you've got."

Morris would have liked that. With his anger, his hatred of modern civilization, and his passionate plea for high standards, he may have begun by burning. But he started a fire that lit up the world.

RIGHT John Ruskin (centre) with William Bell-Scott (left) and the poet and painter Dante Gabriel Rossetti (right). Ruskin's *The Stones of Venice* (1851–3), in which he attacked the "accurate mouldings" and "perfect polishings" that characterized middle-class interiors in an industrial age, marked a turning point in the history of design.

RED HOUSE

Philip Webb for William Morris, 1859–60

Red House at Bexleyheath in Kent is one of the most famous of all Victorian buildings, for a variety of reasons. Its unassuming, faintly vernacular character marks a shift away from the Gothic Revival's preoccupation with fussy ostentation and historicism – "a quiet revolution," in the words of Sir Hugh Casson. It was the first building to be designed by Philip Webb (1831–1915), the greatest and most highly principled of all the Arts and Crafts architects. And its owner was William Morris.

Red House was conceived in the summer of 1858, during a boating trip in France that Morris made with Webb and Charles Faulkner, an old friend from Oxford. "Topsy," as Morris was affectionately known, was then twenty-four with £780 (about $1,250) a year and confused ideas about how he wanted to spend the rest of his life. The influence of Ruskin had led him to reject a plan to enter the Church in favour of architecture and a spell of training in the Oxford office of the architect G. E. Street. It was here that Morris had first met Webb, who was Street's senior draughtsman. Then, when the tedium of office life became too much, he had turned to a more bohemian life in London, learning the painter's craft from Dante Gabriel Rossetti. He was also a published poet, although *The Defence of Guinevere*, his first volume of verse, met an unenthusiastic response when it appeared in the spring of 1858. Even Ruskin seemed unsure of its curious blend of Arthurian romance and anguished sexual repression, saying that the poems were "very, very great indeed – in their own peculiar way."

Morris's private income, inherited from his father, meant he didn't have to worry too much about settling down and earning a living. But he had just become engaged to Janey Burden, an Oxford stable hand's daughter whom he had met while she was posing for Rossetti; they were to be married the following year, and this – and Janey's need to distance herself from her plebeian origins – provided the impetus for the building of a country home where the newly-weds could set up house.

So it was that, as Morris rowed down the river to Abbeville and Amiens, Webb sketched out some rough designs for his new house on the back of one of the maps in their guidebook. On returning to England, Morris and his architect travelled around in search of a suitable location, and eventually hit upon the hamlet of Upton, near Bexleyheath. Webb's designs for Red House were finished by April 1859. Contracts were signed the following month, and in the late summer of 1860 the Morrises moved in.

"I wish you could see the house which Morris (who has money) has built for himself in Kent," wrote Rossetti to a friend. "It is a most noble work in every way, and more a poem than a house... but an admirable place to live in too."

LEFT **Philip Webb, who designed Red House for William Morris, is today regarded as the finest exponent of Arts and Crafts architecture. He first met Morris while working as senior draughtsman in the Oxford office of the architect G. E. Street. The two remained friends until Morris's death in 1896.**

RIGHT **Red House, showing the covered well that Webb himself designed. It is one of the few concessions to embellishment in the austere façade, another being the fenestration. In this view, bull's eye windows can be seen directly above tall, slender casements and pointed arches.**

The poem, in the rich red brick and tile for which it was named, is roughly L-shaped, with steeply pitched roofs and a staircase tower nestling in the inner angle. The entrance façade is restrained to the point of severity, broken by a projecting gabled porch which adds to the solemnity rather than relieving it. The whole thing is reminiscent of the earnest High Church parsonages built in the 1850s by Webb's teacher, Street, and William Butterfield, the only contemporary architect whose work he took the trouble to sketch. Webb's sole concession to embellishment is the fenestration: there are tall, slender casements, six openings high; bull's eyes with leaded panes; wide four-pane by three-pane sashes with shallow segmental heads; windows recessed in pointed tympanums with pointed relieving arches. Webb's Puginesque intention was to have the various elements of the building declare their function externally without using extraneous ornament. It can be bewildering, making one want to know exactly what is going on inside to justify such a variety of openings.

And what was going on when Morris took possession of Red House was a frenzy of activity. When it came to furnishing and decorating the conjugal home, he had to grapple with his Ruskinian distaste for poor contemporary design and meretricious ornament. Nothing suitable could be found: according to J. W. Mackail, his authorized biographer (and the son-in-law of Edward Burne-Jones), "not a chair or table, or a bed; not a cloth or paper hanging for the walls; nor a curtain nor a candlestick; nor a jug to hold wine or a glass to drink it out of, but had to be re-invented." This act of re-invention, so crucial for the subsequent history of the Arts and Crafts

BELOW The first-floor drawing room, showing the huge wooden settle brought by Morris from his London lodgings. Webb converted it into a sort of minstrel gallery, adding a ladder and a balustrade. The murals are based on a fourteenth-century romance by Jean Froissart and are partly the work of Edward Burne-Jones.

ABOVE **The staircase and upper landing. The decoration of Red House was a collaborative effort in which everyone – William and Janey Morris, their friends and relations – played a part. Weekend house guests were frequently called on to earn their keep in this way.**

movement, involved family and like-minded friends not only in designing, but actually in making the interiors. Inevitably, medieval themes abounded. Morris and Janey worked together on hangings and embroideries, enlisting the aid of Janey's sister Bessie, who helped to create a series of appliqués based on Chaucer's *Legend of Good Women*. Burne-Jones painted tiles and began a series of murals for the first-floor drawing room based on Jean Froissart's romance of Sire Degrevaunt and depicting the Morrises as king and queen at a wedding feast. Working parties of friends pricked bold geometrical designs on the plaster of the ceilings; even Morris's classmate Faulkner, who was no artist, was called on to play his part in this when he came to stay. Much of the furniture, in a simple but rather heavy Gothic-style, was made by

Webb, who also contributed metalwork and tableware. Other pieces were brought in from Morris's old London lodgings, including a colossal settle designed by him and painted by Rossetti with scenes from Dante; it was installed at one end of the drawing room, where Webb converted it into a frankly peculiar version of a medieval screen by adding a minstrel gallery and a ladder, which also gave access to the roofspace.

"It is not an original remark," Morris once said, "but I make it here, that home is where I meet people with whom I sympathize, whom I love." The five years that William Morris spent at Red House were some of the happiest of his life. Each weekend, artistic friends would arrive at the local station to be met by Morris with his horse and cart and brought to the house to work on its decoration, to talk, to smoke their pipes, and while away the summer afternoons playing bowls on the lawn. They also played childish pranks on him, taking in his waistcoat so he thought he had put on weight overnight, or heating up a thermometer to convince him the weather was abnormally warm. The idea of an artistic community, which was to loom so large in the thinking of the Arts and Crafts movement, was something Morris cherished.

Janey Morris, if not exactly besotted with her new husband, had at least not yet fallen into the habit of sleeping with his friends, as she would do for much of their married life. Their first daughter, Jenny, was born at the house in January 1861 – a "little accident which has just befallen Topsy and Mrs T" was how her lover-to-be Rossetti described the event. The couple's second child, May, followed fourteen months later; one of her earliest memories was of scattering rose petals over the poet Algernon Swinburne as he lay dozing in the Red House orchard.

The team of friends who had collaborated on Red House went on to found the firm of Morris, Marshall, Faulkner & Co. Ironically, it was the success of this venture that led the Morris family to leave Red House after only five years. In 1865 the London business, which was originally based in Red Lion Square, moved to larger premises in Bloomsbury, and Morris reluctantly decided that he needed to spend more time at "the Firm." Red House was sold, and Morris, Janey, and the two girls went to live over the business. He never went back.

THE FIRM

The work of Morris & Co.

"Mr Morris has some of his very best [carpets] manufactured in Kidderminster…but we cannot afford Morris, much as we should like to do so, for his Kidderminsters are as costly as most people's Brussels." The wistful note struck by Mrs Panton in her best-selling *Hints for Young Householders* must have found an echo in the hearts of many middle-class newly-weds in the 1890s. Not only the carpets, but virtually everything produced by the most sought-after art furnishers in Britain was an object of desire. Worshippers in cathedrals – Birmingham, Salisbury, Christ Church in Oxford – as well as in hundreds of parish churches from Cornwall to Cumberland could find diversion from interminable sermons by admiring new stained-glass windows supplied by Morris & Co. At the same time in London, aesthetes like James Whistler and Oscar Wilde met regularly in the fashionable Green Dining-room at the South Kensington Museum to exchange *bons mots* in suitably artistic surroundings provided by Morris & Co. Diplomats who came to St James's Palace walked through rooms decorated by Morris & Co. Wealthy industrialists put up with Morris haranguing them, so long as he consented to redesign their homes. Genteel ladies bought his ready-traced patterns for "art needlework" to

BELOW The weaving workshops of Morris & Co. at Merton Abbey. Located on the leafy banks of the River Wandle, near Wimbledon, south London, these pleasant and spacious works were ideologically sound and also highly practical, allowing all the weaving and dyeing facilities to be housed together.

RIGHT An employee of "The Firm," as Morris & Co. was affectionately known, printing chintz with hand blocks at Merton Abbey, where the workshop relocated in 1881. It was here that Morris was able to realize his ambition: to mass-produce hand-dyed, hand-printed textiles that the middle classes could afford.

embroider in the comfort of their boudoirs. Other firms shamelessly copied his designs, and the interiors of prosperous suburban villas all over the country were decked with his style of papers, fabrics, and furniture. As *The Spectator* noted in 1883, "'Morris' has become a household word for all who wish their material surroundings to be beautiful yet appropriate for homely use."

The Firm, as it was colloquially known, began life on 11 April 1861 as Morris, Marshall, Faulkner & Co., "Fine Art Workmen in Painting, Carving, Furniture and the Metals," with premises at 8 Red Lion Square, London. There were initially seven partners: Morris himself; the painters Dante Gabriel Rossetti, Edward Burne-Jones, and Ford Madox Brown; the architect Philip Webb; Peter Paul Marshall, a surveyor and sanitary engineer who was friendly with Brown; and Charles Faulkner, an academic and an old friend of Morris and Burne-Jones from their student days in Oxford. In its prospectus, the Firm modestly declared that decorative art had reached a point "at which it seems desirable that Artists of reputation should devote their time to it"; and announced that this was what the partners intended to do. Since they were able to undertake "any species of decoration, mural or otherwise, from pictures, properly so-called, down to the

consideration of the smallest work susceptible of art beauty," they offered a wide range of services and products, including mural decoration, architectural carving, stained glass, metalwork and jewellery, furniture, and embroidery.

Work by Morris, Marshall, Faulkner & Co. was first shown to the public in the Medieval Court at the International Exhibition of 1862, where the Firm sold £150 (about $240) of goods, won two medals of commendation, and caused a minor storm — which did its reputation no harm at all — when other exhibitors accused the partners of touching up old stained glass and passing it off as their own creation. Orders for glass followed, notably from the architect G. F. Bodley, who commissioned work for a series of new churches, beginning with St Michael's, Brighton, and All Saints, Selsey. For most of the 1860s, stained glass, designed by Rossetti, Brown, Burne-Jones, and Webb, was the Firm's main product. (In one year alone — 1866 — it accounted for seventy-seven per cent of total sales.) At the same time, however, the partners continued to produce the range of items offered in their prospectus. Most of the furniture was designed by Webb in a sort of heavy Red House Gothic-style, using oak either stained black or green, or elaborately decorated by Burne-Jones or Morris.

Webb also designed metalwork, table glass, and jewellery. Faulkner and his two sisters painted tiles, and Morris, his wife Janey, and sister-in-law Bessie all worked embroidered panels and hangings, along with Burne-Jones's wife Georgiana and Mrs Campfield, wife of the works' foreman. The first of the famous wallpapers was "Trellis," designed in November 1862 with climbing roses by Morris and birds by Webb, and hand-printed from pearwood blocks. However, the first to go on sale to the public was actually "Daisy," which outsold all the Firm's other papers for half a century. Red Lion Square was no home-spun cottage industry of the sort beloved by the Arts and Crafts movement in the 1920s and 1930s. Manufacture was usually farmed out to others: much of Webb's furniture, for example, was made by a local cabinet-maker named Curwen. Table glass was produced by Powell & Son of Whitefriars, while Jeffrey & Co. of Islington printed the Firm's wallpapers.

In spite of periodic cash crises, the enterprise prospered, moving into new premises at 26 Queen Square, Bloomsbury, in 1865 and opening separate showrooms in Oxford Street in 1877, two years after the partnership had been dissolved and reconstituted as Morris & Co. with William Morris as sole proprietor. In 1881 the business moved again, to an old silk-weaving factory at Merton Abbey in south London, where Morris was able to bring textile production, which had previously been farmed out to a number of manufacturers, under his own control. Of the original partners, only Morris, Webb, and Burne-Jones continued to provide designs. Other key

ABOVE A rush-seated Sussex chair shown in front of Morris's "Iris" wallpaper design. One of the company's best-known products, the popular Sussex seating range was based on eighteenth-century vernacular furniture. A model similar to this example was advertised for sale at nine shillings (about seventy cents).

LEFT A cabinet designed by George Jack (1855–1932), Webb's assistant from 1880. Jack's designs were influenced by more sophisticated eighteenth-century styles than those favoured by Morris. They were often constructed in mahogany or other expensive hardwoods, and used complex techniques such as marquetry.

figures in the Firm's heyday during the 1880s and 1890s included J. H. Dearle, who joined in 1878 and contributed designs for textiles and wallpapers, eventually becoming art director; Webb's assistant George Jack, who was the chief furniture designer in the 1890s; and Morris's daughter May, who took over embroidery in 1885 and also designed papers and jewellery. In addition, the Firm sold work produced by others, notably the light fittings and metalwork of W. A. S. Benson (see page 29) and the pottery and tiles of William de Morgan.

Morris & Co.'s impact on contemporary taste was considerable – so much so that, by the 1880s, it was reckoned that "nearly all the better kind of designs in the shops are, as far as they are good, cribs from Morris, just altered sufficiently to prevent unpleasantness." By this time, output had moved a long way from the medievalized work of the early years, towards a much lighter style that drew its inspiration from the late seventeenth and early eighteenth centuries. To a wealthy middle class which was, like Morris himself, reacting against the decorative arts of its parents' generation, Morris's designs came as a breath of fresh air.

In 1897, the year after Morris's death, the designer and illustrator Walter Crane described the change in public taste wrought by his friend. The Sussex chair, with its rush seat and frame of ebonized wood, had replaced "the wavy-backed and curly-legged stuffed chair" of the mid-century, with its "concealed, and often very unreliable, construction." Plain or stained floorboards were covered with bordered oriental rugs and fringed Axminsters; walls were given "rich, or simple, flat patterns [which] acknowledged the wall, and expressed the proportions of the room." Interior woodwork was painted white or green instead of being marbled or grained; curtains that matched the coverings or complemented the colours of the room were hung on slender black wood or light brass curtain rods, displacing "the heavy mahogany and ormolu battering-rams, with their fringed and festooned upholstery, which had hitherto overshadowed the window of the so-called comfortable classes." Display cabinets filled with Dresden and Sèvres gave way to blue-and-white Nanking and Delft; plain oak trestle tables banished heavy mahogany; and "the deep, high-backed, canopied settee with loose cushions ousted the castored and padded couch from the fireside."

ABOVE **The Vyner Memorial window (1872) by Edward Burne-Jones, one of several Morris & Co. designs installed in Christ Church Cathedral, Oxford. A founding partner in the Firm, Burne-Jones produced many designs for stained glass, which dominated the company's output in its early years.**

Crane characterized these changes in terms that might be a manifesto for the whole Arts and Crafts movement: "…a revival of the medieval spirit (not the letter) in design; a return to simplicity, to sincerity; to good materials and sound workmanship; to rich and suggestive surface decoration, and simple constructive forms."

The Firm continued to operate after Morris's death, but its reputation as one of the nation's leading art furnishers declined from the 1920s, its lines beginning to appear old-fashioned. Other companies, such as Liberty and Heal & Son (see page 134), adopted its high standards but designed cheaper, more modern furnishings that took advantage of the latest industrial production methods. Morris & Co. struggled on until May 1940, when it finally went into liquidation.

CRAGSIDE

Richard Norman Shaw for William Armstrong, 1869–84

LEFT A vaguely lyrical evocation of an equally vague past, the exterior of Cragside comprises many different elements, rising and falling in an eclectic range of historical styles. In this view, dramatic tension is created by juxtaposing mullioned bay windows and tall Tudor chimneys with a Gothic arch.

lthough Webb's Red House (see page 14) can fairly claim to be the first house of the Arts and Crafts movement, it was the work of another, very different architect that had a more immediate appeal to the industrialists and professional men who formed the core of the movement's client base. By no stretch of the imagination could Richard Norman Shaw (1831–1912) be called an Arts and Crafts architect. He was too much of a showman to share Webb's desire for simple, honest building – he once described Webb as "a very able man indeed, but with a strong liking for the ugly" – and he was too ambitious for wealth and status to accept the notion of the architect as just another craftsman, as promoted by Morris, "a great man who somehow delighted in glaring wallpapers." But the eclectic, unhistorical, and supremely picturesque style evolved by Shaw

and his friend William Eden Nesfield (1835–88) in a string of tile-hung and timber-framed country houses, lodges, and cottages in the 1860s was more influential than Red House in banishing the earnest pedantries of the Gothic Revival. What it lacked in respect for the vernacular, "Old English," as the style was known, more than made up for in visual appeal; its ability to combine quaintness with modern comfort struck just the right note with patrons seeking to legitimize their wealth by anchoring it to an attractively vague past. Old English and new money were made for each other. Cragside in Northumberland is a wonderful example of Old English at its most exuberant. The client was the armaments tycoon William Armstrong, who in 1863 had built himself a rather ordinary villa as a weekend retreat on a spectacular site overlooking the Debdon valley, twenty miles or so north of his home at Jesmond Dene in Newcastle-upon-Tyne. In 1869 Shaw was commissioned to add a new gallery to Jesmond Dene, and shortly afterwards Armstrong invited him to produce a scheme for enlarging the villa, which was called Cragside. Over the next fifteen years he more than tripled its size, beginning with a new inner hall, dining room, and library, installing hot-air, plunge, and shower baths beneath and bedrooms above. When these works were nearing completion, Armstrong decided he needed more space, so Shaw created a new wing to the south of the main block, containing a staircase and long gallery, and the Gilnockie Tower, based on the stronghold of his client's supposed ancestor, John Armstrong of Gilnockie, a border raider hanged by James V of Scotland in 1530. Shaw also raised the tower of the original house and crowned it with a half-timbered gable. From 1883 to 1885 yet another wing was added; it housed a large top-lit drawing room that doubled as a gallery for Armstrong's collection of contemporary art.

Critics were uneasy about the lack of cohesion, stating that it looked as if "two or three houses had been brought together." But much of Cragside's magic stems from this lack of cohesion. Gables jostle with crenellations; towers strive to outreach tall Tudor chimneystacks; cavernous Gothic arches compete with mullioned bay windows; and half-timbering stands next to dressed ashlar and rough stonework. There is no attempt at historical accuracy, no reverence for vernacular tradition — just an exhilaration at breaking free from the shackles of the early-Victorian style wars, a refusal to imitate any one historical style. Such liberal romanticism was fully in tune with the products, if not the theories, of the Arts and Crafts movement.

By the end of the nineteenth century, Shaw had moved away from Cragside's eclecticism towards the more grandiose formality of the "Wrenaissance", distancing himself further from Morris, Webb, and their circle. But, the young Arts and Crafts architects who came after him owed him more than he, or they, would care to admit.

BELOW The top-lit drawing room, which Shaw added to the original house in 1883–5 and which also served as a gallery for William Armstrong's growing collection of pictures. The monumental inglenook that dominates the room was the work of W. R. Lethaby, Shaw's chief assistant.

ANTI-SCRAPE

The Society for the Protection of Ancient Buildings

En route from Kelmscott to Broadway in the Cotswolds in September 1876, William Morris was appalled to see that the medieval church of St John the Baptist in Burford was being stripped of its patina of age as it underwent a drastic "restoration" at the hands of his old employer, G. E. Street. He remonstrated with the vicar, only to be told, "The church, Sir, is mine; and if I choose to, I shall stand on my head in it." Undeterred, he began to mull over the idea of forming a pressure group to campaign against such insensitive restoration work; and when, on a visit to Tewkesbury the following spring, he found that George Gilbert Scott was subjecting the old abbey to the same treatment as Burford church, he fired off an impassioned letter to *The Athenaeum*: "Is it altogether too late to do something to save it – it and whatever else of beautiful is still left us of the sites of the ancient buildings…?"

It was indeed too late for Tewkesbury Abbey, but others heeded his plea in *The Athenaeum* for "an association for the purposes of watching over and protecting these relics," and in 1878 the Society for the Protection of Ancient Buildings (SPAB) was formed. Morris was its secretary and, in a gesture that showed the Firm was prepared to put its money where its proprietor's mouth was, Morris & Co. refused to take any more stained-glass commissions from churches under restoration.

The SPAB (which is still going strong over 120 years later) met with plenty of opposition – much of it, predictably, from architects specializing in church restoration and from the clergy who commissioned them. The group was lampooned as "Anti-scrape" because of its antagonism to the practice of scraping weathered stone to make it smooth and characterless; its members were castigated for preferring to see ancient buildings

crumble to dust and for over-emphasizing the Gothic at the expense of other architectural styles. But Morris's plea struck a chord with the Victorian intelligentsia. By the early 1890s the Society boasted over 400 members. There were the usual suspects — friends and colleagues like Philip Webb and George Jack, Burne-Jones, William de Morgan, Walter Crane, W. A. S. Benson, and, of course, John Ruskin, from whom the Society took its battle cry: "Do not let us talk then of restoration: the thing is a lie from beginning to end." But emerging young Arts and Crafts designers, including W. R. Lethaby, Ernest Gimson, Detmar Blow, and C. R. Ashbee, were also drawn to the cause. And the Society was packed with establishment figures: society painters such as Holman Hunt, Lawrence Alma-Tadema, and G. F. Watts; writers and poets like Thomas Carlyle, Thomas Hardy, Coventry Patmore, and Robert Bridges; Leslie Stephen, the first editor of the *Dictionary of National Biography*, and Sir John Lubbock, the Liberal Member of Parliament responsible for the passing of the first Ancient Monuments Act in 1882.

The SPAB's early preoccupation with the fate of churches and the perils of over-restoration soon spilled over into more general lobbying for the preservation of all historic buildings. Largely because the same people were involved, the SPAB and the early Arts and Crafts movement were both manifestations of a hatred of modern civilization, and a nostalgia for a largely mythical, pre-industrial past, which was heroic but ultimately hopeless. But one could argue that the formation of Antiscrape was William Morris's most enduring contribution to national culture. The SPAB virtually invented the notion of a national architectural heritage. It promoted a set of architectural and social values that were adopted by a whole new generation of designers. And in so doing, it helped to define an ideal that is still potent today.

WIGHTWICK MANOR

Edward Ould for S. T. Mander, 1887–8, 1893

Samuel Theodore Mander (1853–1900) was the archetypal Morris & Co. client. A liberal with a well-honed sense of social responsibility, he served his community as a magistrate, councillor, and eventually as mayor of Wolverhampton; he was chairman of the school board, a lay preacher, a temperance reformer, and a member of various local committees. As a director of the family firm of Mander Brothers, successful manufacturers of paints and varnishes, he was in a position to afford Morris & Co.'s products. And he believed in Ruskin and Art. A copy of *The Stones of Venice* was on his bookshelf, and when he went in 1884 to hear Oscar Wilde lecture on "The House Beautiful," he diligently wrote down in his notebook the "Rules in Art" which Wilde had happily plagiarized from Morris, such as "Do not use anything which you do not know to be a pleasure to yourself and which you do not believe was a pleasure to the workman who made it."

In 1887 Mander and his wife Flora (whose maiden name, rather improbably, was Paint) decided to desert their semi-detached villa in Wolverhampton and move to a small country estate

BELOW Wightwick Manor, the work of the architect Edward Ould, was part of a late-Victorian revival of interest in timber-framed buildings, whose influence was felt particularly in the north-west of England.

at Wightwick, three miles west of the town. The seventeenth-century brick house they acquired with the estate was not considered suitable as a family home, however, so the Manders commissioned an entirely new house, remodelling the old building as staff accommodation and removing some of the choicer pieces of panelling for re-use elsewhere. Their architect was Edward Ould of the Liverpool and Chester firm of Grayson & Ould — not perhaps among the first rank of contemporary designers, but competent enough and, more to the point, a respected authority on timber-framed houses. He played a leading role in the resurgence of black-and-white architecture in the north-west of England, producing a number of Tudoresque timber-framed villas in the area, mainly for industrialists like Mander. "Given a suitable client," he wrote, "one who is worthy of the privilege of living in a timber house... it is an eminently suitable style. ... No style of building will harmonize so quickly and so completely with its surroundings and so soon pass through the crude and brand-new period...."

Ould found his "suitable client" in Theodore Mander. Work started on Wightwick in 1887, and the family moved in the following year. The house, a picturesque mixture of carved oak and moulded terracotta, local sandstone, brick, and tile, was not particularly large. Nor did it need to be — it was a manufacturer's villa on the outskirts

of town rather than a full-fledged country house. But by 1893, the Manders' social ambitions had grown along with their family. (Of their four children, two had been born since their move.) Ould was brought back to add a new wing with five guest rooms — there had been none in the original house — a huge living hall called the Great Parlour, and a new billiard room and dining room. At the same time, the dining room in the 1887 wing was converted into a library.

The later work is more confident, more scholarly, and more richly decorated. The expanses of rather garish Ruabon brickwork give way to a softer and less obtrusive base course of local sandstone, encouraging the eye to dwell on the intricate oak carving above, which was made by the Cambridge firm of Rattee & Kett. Deliberate period quotes abound. The oriel on the east front was copied from Little Moreton Hall in Cheshire; the fifteenth-century Ockwells Manor in Buckinghamshire provided the inspiration for the barge boards and the dormer on the garden front; the lead rainwater heads were copied from Tudor examples at Haddon Hall in Derbyshire.

Theodore and Flora Mander turned naturally to Morris & Co. for many of the furnishings of their new house. Thirteen rooms were hung with Morris wallpapers and textiles. "Larkspur," an attractive design of blue larkspur, pink blossom, and buff roses dating from the 1870s, was used in the library. And most of the guest rooms still have the names they acquired from their original Morris decoration — Honeysuckle, Acanthus, Daisy, and Pomegranate.

However, the Manders did not commission Morris & Co. to decorate their house; like many of the Firm's clients, they simply ordered particular items that appealed to them — not only papers and fabrics, but also tiles, light fittings, and Georgian reproduction furniture of the type popular in the early 1890s. These were mixed with seventeenth-, eighteenth-, and nineteenth-century pieces they had acquired elsewhere.

The only professional decorator known to have been involved was Charles Eamer Kempe, best remembered today as a designer of stained glass. In 1888 the Manders had commissioned him to produce glass panels for their entrance hall, representing Fortitude, Abundance, Peace, Industry, Joy, and Temperance — all attributes

Theodore seems to have possessed in plenty, although the Joy may have been tempered by the Temperance. When the new wing was built in 1893, Kempe was brought in to advise on the decoration of the two-storey-high Great Parlour, a masterly reinterpretation of a Tudor hall, complete with screens, minstrel gallery, and exposed roof timbers boldly picked out in a polychromatic pattern of red, gold, green, and black. The Parlour is in reality a living hall of the type popularized in the 1860s by Richard Norman Shaw and William Eden Nesfield. A huge inglenook and oak panelling, some of it re-used from the old house, give warmth and a sense of solidity, while the upper walls are filled with panels of J. H. Dearle's "Diagonal Trail" (a brand-new design in 1893) and, above them, a brightly coloured Jacobethan plaster frieze by Kempe depicting the story of Orpheus and Eurydice. "Such a room," wrote the architect Hermann Muthesius in 1904, "offers an impression of beauty, it bids welcome to those who enter, to those who linger in it it gives a feeling of space and, as an all-purpose room, a sense of freedom and informality." Indeed it does.

"Art is the only serious thing in the world," said Oscar Wilde. But no matter how artistic the Manders' tastes, they would have found such a notion blasphemous. Wightwick's message is one of God-fearing, Old English hospitality, and lest anyone forget it, it is reinforced by texts placed in prominent positions both inside and outside the house. The gables are adorned with a suitable quotation from *Troilus and Cressida* — "Welcome ever smiles, and farewell goes out sighing" — and lines from Herrick's Arcadian love lyric, "To Phyllis": "Live, live with me, and thou shalt see/ The pleasures I'll prepare for thee:/What sweets the country can afford/Shall bless thy Bed and bless thy Board./Thy feasting tables shall be hills/ With daisies spread and daffodils." A quote from Ruskin's *Modern Painters* appears in the panelling of the drawing room, while the Great Parlour strikes a more earnest note. The inglenook declares that "A welcoming home puts its faith in God," and Kempe's stained glass includes that perennial Victorian favourite: "Except the Lord build the house they labour in vain that build it." Even the schoolroom, converted from a seventeenth-century malthouse, has a Latin inscription that translates as "Work is a pleasure in itself" — a thoroughly Ruskinian attitude, although one doubts if the Mander children appreciated the sentiment.

Theodore Mander didn't live to see those children grow to adulthood. In September 1900, a few weeks after the Duke and Duchess of York (later George V and Queen Mary) had paid a visit to Wightwick, he died at the house, aged just forty-seven. Flora followed him five years later.

Today the interiors of Wightwick seem even more of a homage to Morris and his circle than they did when Theodore and Flora furnished the house. Their son and daughter-in-law were among the first serious collectors of Pre-Raphaelite art, and from the 1930s onwards Sir Geoffrey and Lady Mander not only acquired a remarkable collection of paintings and drawings from the period, including works by Rossetti, Holman Hunt, Burne-Jones, and Ford Madox Brown, but also brought to the house some fine late-Victorian ceramics, including lustreware by William de Morgan, and stained glass, textiles, furniture, and hand-knotted carpets from William Morris. The collections have also been augmented by Wightwick's current owners, The National Trust.

STANDEN

Philip Webb for James Beale, 1891–4, 1898

Standen was built for James Samuel Beale (1840–1912), a Birmingham solicitor whose family firm had done extremely well out of the rising fortunes of its most prestigious client, the Midland Railway. When the Midland opened its London terminus at St Pancras in 1868, Beale & Co. decided they needed an office in the capital, and James Beale moved down to run it. He and his wife Margaret bought a large detached villa in the fashionable district of Holland Park, Kensington, where they set about raising seven children and James spent his time doing what lawyers do best – making money. By 1890 he was fifty and in a position to think about acquiring a small country estate, initially as a weekend retreat, but ultimately as a place where he could ride, shoot, and play golf in his retirement. So in that year the Beales bought Great Holly-bush, Standen, and Stone, three adjacent farms on the Sussex Weald, two miles south of East Grinstead and within easy reach of London via the railway. The farmhouse at Standen was little more than a cottage (it was demolished six years later), and they decided to build their new house at Great Hollybush – although, rather confusingly, the estate quickly became known as Standen. Almost immediately they fixed on a site and com-missioned the London garden designer G. B. Simpson to lay out the grounds surrounding it, while they looked around for an architect.

ABOVE Standen from the south-east. The blocky, roughcast water tower has the effect of anchoring the house to its landscape, forming a solid fixed point around which the rest of the building pivots.

ABOVE RIGHT James Samuel Beale, the owner of Standen. In this portrait by Sir William Nicholson, Beale looks every inch the rather pompous Victorian professional. The influence of his wife Margaret seems to have played a large part in his choice of Webb as an architect at Standen, and in the use of "advanced" Arts and Crafts decoration throughout the house.

By the following spring, James and Margaret had chosen Philip Webb. They probably came across his name in the homes of their Holland Park neighbours: in 1880, for example, the financier Alexander Ionides, who lived across the road, had commissioned Morris & Co. to undertake a complete redecoration of his house; both Webb and his chief assistant George Jack were involved. Webb had also designed several houses in the neighbourhood during the 1860s, including 1 Holland Park Road for the artist Val Prinsep in 1864, and 1 Palace Green for George Howard, later 9th Earl of Carlisle, in 1868. In addition, Beale was friendly with Sir John Tomes, the Queen's dentist, for whom the architect had built Upwood Gorse near Caterham, also in 1868. When James and Margaret took Webb down to Great Hollybush to look at the site on 11 April 1891, they knew his work; they knew his considerable reputation for high-mindedness and high standards. If they expected him to produce something different from the bland rural retreats that were appearing in the late 1880s and early 1890s, as the rapidly expanding rail network gave London businessmen and their families easy access to the countryside of Sussex and Kent, they were not to be disappointed.

More than thirty years separate Standen from Webb's designs for Red House (see page 14) – and a lot more. For one thing, his feeling for the English rural landscape had grown into a quiet passion. As Lethaby once said, "To Webb, the fields and old buildings of England were a question of quite

religious moment." His response to the trees and old farm buildings that surrounded the Beales' proposed site was to preserve as many of them as possible. An old walnut immediately to the north of the house was marked on the plans at the outset, and both the seventeenth-century weather-boarded barn and the original Hollybush farm-house, an attractive medieval tile-hung building roofed with Horsham sandstone, were retained to form two sides of an open green to the north-west of the main house.

Webb's style had also become much more relaxed and informal since the early days of his career, and there is an apparent simplicity about Standen that belies the enormous amount of art that went into the design. The house epitomizes one of his favourite sayings: "I never begin to be satisfied until my work looks commonplace." His choice of materials managed to convey the idea that the Beales' new house was peculiarly at home in the landscape, without ever pretending to be anything other than a new country residence. In the entrance court, a roughcast water tower stands between tall brick chimneystacks at the junction of the service wing and the main block, both of which are built of mellow, yellow-grey Horsham brick, with rubbed red Keymer bricks used for the window surrounds. But whereas the ground floor of the service wing is topped with a series of weatherboarded gables, the main block also uses stone for the stringcourse, the porch, and the projecting bay next to it (added in 1898, after the Beales decided that the original entrance hall was too small). The south front, where the principal living rooms – the morning room, dining room, and drawing room – take advantage of the views over the Medway valley, is even more complex. The ground floor is of locally quarried stone, although the white, segmental sash windows still have redbrick dressings; above them flat-headed sashes, again with brick dressings, punctuate the tile-hung first floor. And the ensemble is topped with five more weatherboarded gables with roofs of clay tiles that project forward from the lime-washed water tower on one side and a single-storey conservatory with a glazed roof on the other.

This shouldn't work. It ought to be a hopeless muddle of architectural references. But the reticence of the design, the easy informality of the composition and, above all, Webb's ability to work with his materials while never relinquishing control, make Standen a supremely attractive house. There is no fakery, no historicist attempt to deceive one into thinking that the building has grown piecemeal over the centuries, there is just an honest joy in the past.

Standen's interiors suggest that neither the architect nor his clients wanted any of the heavy Gothic work found at Red House, or the elaborate Jacobean plasterwork and polychromatic ornament of Wightwick. Instead, plain plaster ceilings and simple panelled walls give the principal rooms the air of an unpretentious early-Georgian country house. The bold abstract geometry of the chimney-pieces, with their occasional echoes of Vanbrugh – arguably the finest work of Webb's career – are the only self-indulgence, and even here their modest scale accords with the unassuming architecture.

Building work at Standen, which cost the considerable sum of £18,065 (roughly $28,900) including Webb's £820 ($1,312) fee, was finished by August 1894, and the Beales turned to the task of furnishing the house. All the wallpapers were supplied by Morris & Co. but, in keeping with the overall atmosphere, the family seems to have preferred the Firm's earlier, less elaborate designs – "Sunflower" in the drawing room, "Trellis" in several of the ground-floor corridors, "Bachelor's Button" for the staircase and the passage upstairs, "Larkspur" and "Willow" in the bedrooms. Margaret Beale also ordered several Morris chintzes for hangings and curtains: J. H. Dearle's "Daffodil" was hung in the morning room, and

"Severn" and "African Marigold" were used in other parts of the house. Margaret and her daughters were accomplished needlewomen in their own right, and in the best Morris tradition they made their own hangings by embroidering versions of several Morris designs, including "Artichoke" (see below),"Pomegranate," and "Vine." W. A. S. Benson provided light fittings and lamps (the house was designed for electric lighting from the outset). The furniture, apart from a number of built-in cupboards and dressers by Webb, was an eclectic mix of up-to-date Georgian Revival pieces from the Morris catalogue, designed by George Jack; rather grander items from other well-known art furnishers such as Collinson & Lock and S. & J. Jewell; and more ordinary beds and tables bought at the retailers Heal's and Maple's.

In spite of such self-consciously artistic interiors, which one suspects owed much to Margaret Beale and her Holland Park neighbours, both the architecture and the decoration of Standen represent a move away from the quaint "House Beautiful" clutter of the previous decades. There is a new purity about the house, a lightness of touch that bears witness not only to the disdain felt by Webb in later life for "the modern furnisher who, in these days of the art dilettante, chokes up space as if it were a thing offensive," but also to his genius for transcending his age and making something entirely new out of his love for the past. As the twentieth century dawned, lesser talents would continue to lose themselves in the byways of history; those who didn't owed much of their success to the example of Webb at Standen.

LEFT This silk hanging in the North Bedroom at Standen was worked by Margaret Beale and her three eldest daughters in about 1896. The design is Morris's "Artichoke." The original colours have been somewhat faded by sunlight.

MELSETTER HOUSE

W. R. Lethaby for Thomas Middlemore, 1898

Dreams of an escape from the industrial society that had made their fortune loomed large in the thinking of many late-Victorian manufacturers. They pictured a retreat into the mythical stained-glass past they had read about in *The Defence of Guinevere* or *The Idylls of the King*, or into the equally mythical Eden of the English countryside. But few went as far in realizing this ambition as Thomas Middlemore, who sold his leather business in Birmingham in 1896 and fled 400 miles north to the Orkneys. There, on a secluded site nestling against a hillside and looking out over the Pentland Firth to the Scottish mainland, he built Melsetter House.

Middlemore was another archetypal Arts and Crafts client – rich, romantic, and radical. His family firm had done well under his father, who had acquired some lucrative defence contracts, and it prospered still further after Thomas took over the management in 1868 and set up a factory in Coventry to make bicycle saddles. By the time he inherited the concern outright on the death of his father in 1889, Thomas was a very wealthy man, and he and his wife Theodosia were prominent in Birmingham's advanced artistic and political circles. His younger brother, a Liberal MP, collected paintings by Holman Hunt and Burne-Jones, and his sister wrote earnest tracts on

ABOVE **Melsetter House. Romantically located on Hoy, one of the Orkney Islands off the north coast of Scotland, the house was described by William Morris's daughter May as "a sort of fairy palace on the edge of the great northern seas."**

Christian Socialism. Theodosia exhibited her embroideries at the Arts and Crafts Exhibition Society's annual shows, ordered furnishings from Morris & Co., and was friendly with May Morris.

But Middlemore wasn't content to live the life of a prosperous Birmingham bourgeois with a comfortable villa in the suburbs and an office in the city. Like many before him, he sought to make the transition from successful industrialist to landed gentleman; although in his case, the social advancement that went along with the purchase of a country seat was tempered by a desire to turn his back on modern society and go in search of an unspoilt rural utopia. In 1896, while still in his fifties, he sold his business and retired to the remote island of Rousay in the Orkneys, a move that may have been prompted by Theodosia, whose family came from Kinlochbervie on the north-west coast of Scotland. Two years later he bought the 40,000-acre Melsetter estate, which was spread over four of the Orkney Islands — Hoy, Walls, Fara, and Rysa. The laird's house on Long Hope Sound at the southern end of Hoy was an austere, low building traditionally constructed from rough-cast sandstone rubble. Its

RIGHT **W. R. Lethaby, Melsetter's architect, preserved parts of the old buildings he found on the site. Where buildings had to be demolished, he re-used many of the structural features, including this roll-moulded doorway.**

core dated from the seventeenth century, but it had been altered and added to over the years until it was surrounded by a motley, but attractive, community of extensions and outbuildings.

The simple life was all very well, but Melsetter House clearly would not do as it stood. Middlemore immediately decided to rebuild, and brought in William Richard Lethaby (1857–1931), an architect with impeccable credentials as a member of the Morris-Webb circle. After working as chief assistant to Richard Norman Shaw for ten years, Lethaby had set up a practice for himself in 1889. He had shown work at the Arts and Crafts Exhibition Society, and lectured to its members. He was on the committee of the Society for the Protection of Ancient Buildings (Morris had himself proposed him for membership), and was a founder-member of the Art-Workers' Guild, a director of the new Central School of Arts and Crafts, a staunch socialist, and an earnest admirer of the aesthetic and political principles of Philip Webb. "In his life I find a means of judging my own," he wrote later. In 1893 he had designed The Hurst, a small country house in Sutton Coldfield which clearly showed his debt to Webb. His client for this house was a friend of the Middlemores, the solicitor Charles Matthews, and it was probably through Matthews that Thomas Middlemore came to approach him.

There is a story that Lethaby's first design for Melsetter, produced in his chambers in Gray's Inn Square, was scrapped after he paid a visit to Hoy and actually saw the rambling collection of buildings he had proposed to sweep away. Old buildings, he said in an SPAB address in 1906, "are survivals, and a land in which they had been carefully conserved would carry on its past in actual being. We want not mere models and abstract shapes of buildings, but the very handiwork of the men of old, and the stones they laid." And true to his SPAB principles, he insisted that as much as possible of the old Melsetter should be preserved. The decision was an important one, since it not only anchored Lethaby's enlargements to the Orcadian past (and, in so doing, gave the Middlemores a satisfactory sense of belonging), but also determined the external appearance of the new work. Admittedly, the remodelling was quite drastic. The farmstead to the west of the house was partly demolished to make way for a

ABOVE **Theodosia Middlemore seated in the dining room inglenook at Melsetter House, in a pose that suggests something of the utopian ideals underlying the family's decision to settle on a remote Scottish island. As she sits gazing into the fire, Theodosia is half soulful Pre-Raphaelite lady, half Orcadian farmer's wife.**

LEFT **The sandstone chimneypiece in the hall, showing the Middlemores' family motto, *Mon Desire Loyalte*, under a heraldic frieze. The five corbels, a rather curious feature, were designed to support candles.**

walled rose garden. The roofline of part of the main house was raised and extensions were added until the little laird's house had been turned into a substantial ten-bedroom mansion, with all the conveniences that a wealthy Victorian family might expect — hall, library, drawing room and dining room, a male domain consisting of gun room and smoking room, a chapel to cater for the family's spiritual needs, and extensive domestic offices in the basement to cater for their physical ones. But externally, at least, the new house paid homage to the vernacular traditions of the neighbourhood. Roughcast sandstone rubble and local red sandstone were used, as they had been for the original house. Various elements from the buildings that had been demolished were re-used — a roll-moulded doorway here, a decorative stone bracket there. A new wing to the east, containing an L-shaped drawing room and master bedroom, was given a crow-stepped gable of the type found on comparable buildings elsewhere in the Orkneys. Only occasionally are there signs of a more modern perspective, and even these are hesitant, almost self-effacing: two little heart-shaped windows placed, rather sweetly, in the gable over the Middlemores' bedroom, with a star and a moon above them; a faintly mystical group of sun, cross, and crescent moon carved above the door to the chapel.

In its interiors, Melsetter has a stripped-down simplicity and light informality that suggest how far the Arts and Crafts movement had come since the misty medievalism of Red House and the early decorative schemes of Morris & Co. Walls are given plain panelling beneath plaster friezes depicting the local flora. Only in the hall does Lethaby's (or perhaps Thomas Middlemore's?) quiet reticence break down. A heavy, sandstone chimneybreast is carved in low relief with family coats of arms and the Middlemore motto, *Mon Desire Loyalte*, and in place of a mantel shelf there are five rather bizarre corbels, evidently designed to take candles, whose flickering light must have added a Gothic touch to the scene on stormy winter nights. Some of the furniture and fittings were ordered from Morris & Co., including lamps, ironwork, carpets, curtains, tapestries, and silk hangings; the rest either came from the Middlemores' Birmingham house or were made (in unstained and scrubbed oak) by a local Kirkwall firm to Lethaby's designs. Unfortunately many of the best pieces were sold after Theodosia died in 1944; several are now in the Victoria and Albert Museum.

Lethaby's other work on the estate included designs for a new farmstead, two shooting lodges, the agent's house, and a number of cottages. He designed only one further country house — High Coxlease in Hampshire (1900) — and effectively gave up his architectural practice in 1901 to concentrate on teaching and writing; it is as the theorist of the later Arts and Crafts movement that he is best remembered.

Thomas and Theodosia seem to have been content in their remote, rural utopia: he hunting, fishing, and generally playing the laird; she working on her embroideries or spinning, sometimes in the company of May Morris, a regular visitor in the early years of the century. A photograph shows the Middlemores standing proudly on the steps outside the drawing room under the heart-shaped windows.

May Morris summed up Melsetter as "a sort of fairy palace on the edge of the great northern seas" — a romantic description, if not altogether an accurate one. Melsetter's charm lies in the fact that there is nothing palatial about it, making the house a perfect antidote to the pompous civic pride of turn-of-the-century Birmingham. And the values it embodies — respect for the past, organic growth, a sympathy for the natural landscape, honest craftsmanship — are positive ones. It is easy to sneer at Thomas Middlemore's dreams of escape, but they are dreams that many of us still share today.

THE ARCHITECT
AT HOME

There is a school of thought that holds that the architect who designs his own home is like the lawyer who defends himself in court. He has a fool for a client.

That's a little unfair, perhaps. But it is certainly true that, until the later nineteenth century at least, the homes of England's greatest architects rarely matched up to the work they did for others. There are exceptions, of course: one thinks of the picturesque East Cowes Castle on the Isle of Wight, which John Nash designed for himself in 1798, and where he died thirty-seven years later; or Goose-pie House at Whitehall and Vanbrugh Castle in Greenwich, the charming fantasies that Sir John Vanbrugh built for himself in 1699 and c.1717, respectively. But East Cowes and Vanbrugh Castle are small change beside, say, Nash's Royal Pavilion at Brighton or Vanbrugh's Blenheim Palace in Oxfordshire. And how could it be otherwise? No matter how successful such architects became,

they could rarely hope to match the resources of their wealthy patrons. Inigo Jones died in quite ordinary lodgings at Somerset House on the Strand, Christopher Wren in a modest house leased from the Crown, in the shadow of Hampton Court.

The Arts and Crafts movement was different. Its finest buildings were small-scale. Livable, affordable homes for the prosperous professional classes were its great strength. Pomp and grandeur were anathema to it. In other words, it specialized in just the sort of houses that someone with the social status of an architect might live in. So not surprisingly, quite a number of Arts and Crafts architects took the opportunity to build Arts and Crafts houses of their own. At Sapperton in Gloucestershire, where the old-world air was still uncorrupted, Ernest Gimson, Ernest Barnsley, and Sidney Barnsley all designed homes for themselves, indulging their passionate belief that, as one Edwardian commentator on the results of

LEFT A contemporary photograph of the dining room at Bloemenwerf, a house designed in 1895 by Henry van de Velde for himself and his family at Uccle in Belgium. Van de Velde, a self-confessed control freak, saw the house as a total project, designing everything from the furnishings to the cutlery. His famous dining room chair appears in this picture, and also on page 43.

ABOVE A detail of
the tiled rooftops and
wood cladding at Eliel
Saarinen's house at
Lake Hvitträsk, near
Helsinki. Saarinen
embraced the principles
of the English Arts and
Crafts movement and
combined them with
details and materials
taken from Finnish
vernacular architecture
in an attempt to create
a distinctively national
architectural style.

their labours put it, "beauty consists in line, proportion, texture, workmanship, and most of all in appropriateness; indulgence in ornament for ornament's sake, in patent decorative mediums, and in mechanical patternings, is among the deadly sins." Such indulgence didn't come cheap: Ernest Barnsley's Upper Dorval House, which was a conversion and extension of an existing cottage using local materials and labour, cost just over £1,700 ($2,720), a considerable sum for a small house in 1902, when a decent cottage could be built for well under £600 ($960).

C. F. A. Voysey's home, the Orchard, built in 1899 in Chorleywood, Hertfordshire, was another example of what an architect could do when unfettered by a whining client. True, Voysey had to make concessions which he would have found hard to take if someone else were footing the bill: the joinery was painted pine rather than his preferred unpolished oak, and there was no money for the oak panelling he usually liked to put into his houses. But he could at least install fittings and furnishings to his own design; he could – and did – come closer to realizing his own personal vision than at any other time in his career.

RIGHT A detail of a writing cabinet at Owlpen
Manor, made by Sidney Barnsley around 1914.
The entire cabinet is illustrated on page 69. Barnsley
lived the Arts and Crafts ideal: a true craftsman,
he personally carried out all the work required to
execute his own designs to the highest standard.

Even before it was finished, the Orchard was written up in the British magazine *Country Life*; in 1901 it was illustrated in *Modern British Domestic Architecture and Decoration* by Charles Holme, and described in loving detail by Voysey himself in *The Architectural Review*. It featured in another British magazine, *The Tatler*, in 1906, and in the American magazine, *The Ideal House*, in 1907. And this publicity brought in clients. Inevitably, there was often an element of self-advertisement behind the construction and decoration of an architect's home: both Henry van de Velde's Bloemenwerf (see opposite and page 42) and Joseph Maria Olbrich's Haus Olbrich at Matildenhöhe (see page 52) were conceived primarily as showcases for their designers' work. But there were often other motives besides a simple desire to show what an architect could do, given the opportunity and the absence of an interfering client. A house could be a political act, a personal affirmation of nationalistic values, like the communal complex built by Gesellius, Lindgren, and Saarinen at Hvitträsk in 1902 (see left and page 56). It could be an act of kindness, like Norman Jewson's heroic salvaging operation at Owlpen Manor (see page 66). And, like Howard Van Doren Shaw's Ragdale (see page 46) and Detmar Blow's Hilles (see page 62), it could be the creation of a good comfortable home for the architect and his family – the best reason of all for designing your own house.

BLOEMENWERF

Henry van de Velde, 1895–6

Adolph Loos once wrote that "the time will come when the furnishing of a prison cell by Professor van de Velde will be considered an aggravation of the sentence."

The Bloemenwerf House (1895–6) in the Brussels suburb of Uccle was the first architectural work of the Belgian designer Henry van de Velde (1863–1957), one of the pioneers of modernism. Like Morris, Behrens, and Le Corbusier, van de Velde originally set out to be a painter, and after studying at the Académie des Beaux-Arts in Antwerp he went in 1884 to Paris, where he

mixed with leading Impressionists and Symbolists. Returning to Antwerp in 1886, he continued to paint, producing pieces that were heavily influenced first by the pointillism of Georges Seurat and later by Van Gogh. He also became involved with Les Vingt, ("The Twenty") a Brussels-based group of avant-garde artists who had close ties with the English Arts and Crafts movement, and particularly with the socialist illustrator and designer Walter Crane, one of the founders of the Arts and Crafts Exhibition Society. From about 1890 onwards, as he absorbed the social and

BELOW **Bloemenwerf (1895–6), in Uccle, a suburb of Brussels, was designed by Henry van de Velde (1863–1957). Conceived both as his home and as a showcase for his work, it draws on familiar themes from northern European rural architecture, which are simultaneously subverted by aggressively modern angles and curves.**

ABOVE **A portrait of van de Velde, who modestly (and not entirely fairly) claimed reponsibility for single-handedly bringing the Art Nouveau style into his native Belgium. His design talents were employed on objects as diverse as buildings, furniture, wallpaper, and even dresses for women.**

aesthetic teachings of Morris and Ruskin, van de Velde began to move away from fine art towards design. He experimented with typography and graphics, creating Gauginesque abstract woodcuts for the Belgian magazine *Van Nu en Struks*, and also with the applied arts, in which his first real essay was the tapestry *Angel Vigil* (1893). His work in these areas shows all the swirling, asymmetrical, curvi-linear forms of early Art Nouveau – a style he later claimed, not altogether accurately, to have introduced single-handedly into Belgium. By the mid-1890s he was designing furniture, wallpapers, metalwork, and even women's dresses.

What van de Velde took from Morris and Ruskin was not so much a specific design vocabulary as a romantic insistence on the moral qualities of design. "Ugliness corrupts not only the eyes, but also the heart and mind", he said – a statement that might have come straight from the pages of Ruskin's *The Stones of Venice* or Morris's *News from Nowhere*. But he went further than his English predecessors, maintaining that good design alone had the power to transform society, and that the individual vision of the artist/designer, rather than a collaborative union of all the arts, was the only way to achieve this transformation. (Although in what was for him a rare instance of self-doubt, van de Velde began to question this idea in 1905, asking, "Do I have this right to impose on the world a taste and a wish which is so personal?") The supremacy of the designer – a notion which was of course attractive to designers, although not necessarily to their clients – stemmed from a deep-seated belief in the unity of design. As van de Velde wrote in 1897 in his essay "On the design and building of modern furniture":

> As far as furniture is concerned, the difference is as follows: a homogeneous piece is preferable to a complex one, a homogeneous room to an unordered, incoherent one. It must be recognized that every room has a principal focal point from which its life emanates and to which all other objects must relate and be subordinate. The various furnishings will be arranged in accordance

RIGHT **One of a set of dining room chairs that van de Velde designed for Bloemenwerf. The taut, curving verticals give the piece a dramatic tension, as though it were about to spring apart – a perfect illustration of his belief that "a line is a force."**

with this newly discovered skeleton of the room, and thenceforth they will be perceived as the living organs of the room and indeed of the whole house.

Recognition came slowly. But in 1894 van de Velde was given the chance to create a quasi-public showcase for his work when he married the wealthy Maria Sèthe. Van de Velde had no independent means of his own, and so the following year Maria's family helped to finance the building of a new home for the couple – Bloemenwerf. This was the chance van de Velde had been waiting for. He had thoroughly assimilated his English contemporaries' emphasis on the home as the most appropriate setting for a revolution in design. Bloemenwerf, like the Red House, was to demonstrate the union of arts and crafts – with one important difference. Whereas Morris, Webb, Burne-Jones, and their friends had worked together and separately at the Red House to produce interiors that achieved their harmony from a shared outlook, van de Velde alone designed both Bloemenwerf and everything in it, right down to the knives and forks with which he and Maria ate their meals.

An early watercolour of the design for the entrance elevation makes Bloemenwerf appear strangely like one of the picturesque *cottages ornés* popular in England in the early nineteenth century. Substitute thatch for the roof tiles, strengthen the rather skinny chimneystacks, and add some lattice windows, and you have a "cottage of gentility" straight out of *Mansfield Park*. This impression is lessened by a first sight of the house as built. For one thing, there are too many curves. No Georgian gentleman would have contemplated the sweeping lines of the window heads or the three hooded gables (which are actually four-sided, but are doing their best to be curves). Even the façade itself sweeps backwards, so that the single-storey porch, crowned with a wide low window beneath the central, half-timbered gable, projects forward boldly, simultaneously inviting one to enter and daring one to disapprove of its unconventionality.

And unconventional the house certainly is. The layout is exciting, even disturbing, but it betrays van de Velde's lack of architectural training. It shows his inability to reconcile the everyday needs of good interior planning with a Big Idea, which in this case is a chamfered, basically octagonal plan-form, broken on one of the chamfers by the projecting bay of the dining room and, further along on the same side, by a second bay, part of the adjoining kitchen. The rooms are grouped around a galleried top-lit hall and this, coupled with the odd asymmetrical plan, leads to unfortunate consequences. Few of the spaces are rectangular: most are five-sided; others are irregular hexagons; and here and there, where polygons meet rather awkwardly, there are triangles and parallelograms. Doors and windows intrude at strange angles. The quiet and understated domesticity that the English Arts and Crafts movement aimed for in its buildings is notably absent.

OPPOSITE **The interiors of Bloemenwerf are simple, workmanlike spaces. In contrast to most English interiors of the time (with the possible exception of those by Voysey and Mackintosh) they are determined not to fall into the pit of historical styles. The polygonal shape of the dining room bears witness to van de Velde's unorthodox approach to spatial planning.**

RIGHT **Although van de Velde was influenced by French and Belgian Art Nouveau, this fireplace surround shows how his own interpretation of the movement's curvilinear forms was restrained.**

But while Bloemenwerf's architecture may be too unsettling, its interiors achieve a much more successful tension in repose. Early photographs show brightly lit, functional rooms, decorated with chevron papers and Art Nouveau friezes, and filled with unornamented furniture that relied on triangular bentwood lines for effect. They also show van de Velde groping towards a new design aesthetic, one that accepted Morris's notion of the importance of good design while rejecting his utopian historicism. To put it another way, they show modernism in the making.

Van de Velde's achievement in creating Bloemenwerf tends to be overshadowed by his later career. In 1900 he left Brussels for Berlin, subsequently taking up a post at the Weimar School of Applied Arts (the forerunner of the Bauhaus), where he taught a generation of German designers to reject the past and look to their own powers of invention. In 1914 he engaged in a very public quarrel with Hermann Muthesius over the future of design, Muthesius advocating the importance of standardization and industrial method, and van de Velde holding to the Arts and Crafts ideal of individual creativity. As it turned out, the future belonged to Muthesius. But Bloemenwerf, in spite of its many faults, suggests that perhaps the future was wrong.

RAGDALE

Howard Van Doren Shaw, 1898

One of the few misfortunes to befall the architect Howard Van Doren Shaw (1869–1926), in the course of an otherwise happy and successful life, was that he practised in Chicago at the same time as Frank Lloyd Wright. Comparisons between the work of the two men are inevitable; and the conservative, complacent Shaw seems staid and derivative beside Wright's passionate, innovative genius.

This verdict isn't altogether fair, although it didn't matter in the slightest to Shaw, whose wealthy clientele, the bastions of Chicago society, provided him with a string of country-house commissions, a good living, and a solid reputation.

(Even in the 1930s his friend and biographer Thomas Talmadge could describe him as "the most highly regarded architect in the sphere of domestic, ecclesiastical, and non-commercial architecture in the Middle West" – as though Wright had never existed.) Those clients wanted good manners and good taste. One later recalled why she and her husband had chosen Shaw. It was because he "didn't do anything queer"; Wright's houses, on the other hand, were "perfectly awful" and looked like gas stations.

The son of a prosperous Chicago dry-goods merchant, Shaw was born in 1869, making him Wright's junior by two years. He graduated from

OPPOSITE TOP **Howard Van Doren Shaw with his grandsons.** Shaw was one of Chicago's most successful establishment architects. His respectable, non-threatening style made him popular with the conservative members of Chicago society.

OPPOSITE BOTTOM The east front of Ragdale, showing the influence of Lutyens and other English exponents of the "cottage" style, whose work Shaw learned to respect on the tours of Surrey he made early in his career. The restrained good taste of Ragdale is sometimes missing from Shaw's commissioned work, in which he was often required to comply with the grander tastes of his wealthy clients.

Yale in 1890 and studied architecture at the Massachusetts Institute of Technology before going abroad for a year to explore the buildings of England, Spain, and Italy. He had spent his vacations from MIT working in the office of William Le Baron Jenney, the father of the skyscraper, who pioneered the use of the load-carrying structural frame. When he returned from Europe, Shaw went into Jenney's practice for a couple of years before branching out on his own, quickly carving out a niche for himself providing Chicago's wealthy business community with country houses, particularly in the exclusive residential suburb of Lake Forest on the shores of Lake Michigan.

Shaw's family connections and Ivy League background enabled him to take his place effortlessly in the life of Chicago's social and business élite. He was a pillar of the local establishment, a staunch Republican, treasurer of the Second Presbyterian Church, trustee of the Art Institute of Chicago, and a member of several gentlemen's clubs and country clubs. In 1893 he married Frances Wells, a Chicagoan from his own socio-economic class. By the time he was thirty-eight, the architectural establishment had made him one of their own, electing him Fellow of the American Institute of Architects; in 1926, the

ABOVE **The Shaws enjoyed the outdoor life at Ragdale, putting on open-air theatricals and making cider in the nearby orchard.** The design of the garden reflects this informal approach to country living, an approach that was promoted by influential British garden designers such as Gertrude Jekyll.

year of his death, the AIA honoured him with their highest award, the Gold Medal.

With such a background, we might expect to see Shaw producing the sort of workmanlike "Bozart" buildings that respectable MIT-trained architects were churning out by the hundred during the 1890s. But that didn't happen. Shaw was, as his obituary in the *Architectural Record* put it, "the most conservative of the rebels, and the most rebellious of the conservatives"; his own small rebellion consisted of a deep and lasting commitment to the ideals and architecture of the English Arts and Crafts movement.

This commitment showed itself in a hands-on approach to the practical side of building. Throughout his life, Shaw felt a joy in manual labour; he was a good carpenter, bricklayer, and stonemason, and because he knew these skills, he was able to talk to the craftsmen he employed on their own terms — and to demand exceptionally high standards from them. More significantly, the country homes he designed for the network of

friends and contacts he made on golf courses and tennis courts, in boardrooms and country-club bars, show a strong English influence. His use of gables, sweeping rooflines, and whitewashed roughcast walls recall early Voysey (although admittedly, without any of Voysey's individual flair — one suspects Shaw would have found individual flair rather vulgar); while Lake Forest commissions such as the Coonley house (1908) and the Lamont house (1924) are reminiscent of Lethaby and Lutyens. The latter was Shaw's great hero, and the romantic Surrey vernacular of Crooksbury and Munstead Wood was something he deliberately tried to re-create in the leafy suburbs of Chicago, referring to photographs and to sketches of Lutyens's early Surrey houses he had made during his visits to England in the 1890s.

The only problem was the tension between the comfortable "English" country homes that Shaw liked to produce and the opulent grandeur demanded by his wealthy clients, whose tastes tended to veer towards the classical. If that was really what they wanted, that was what they got — the two formal Italianate mansions he built in Lake Forest for steel magnate Edward L. Ryerson (in 1906 and 1912) are cases in point — but he was happiest when clients shared his quiet passion for the more modest English country house.

Such tensions didn't apply when it came to Ragdale, the home Shaw built for himself, his parents, and his young family on the Lake Forest farm he bought in 1897. At Ragdale, he had no one to please but himself. The exterior was rendered a creamy white, with the eaves, barge-boards, and other external timbers — all of hewn oak — stained grey black. Doors and window shutters were painted a faded peacock blue, and the sashes themselves were white. The outline of the main façade to the east, a projecting central section flanked by two gables, is thoroughly English in its reticence. It recalls nothing so much as the compact country "cottages" produced by Lutyens in the early 1900s — Homewood in Hertfordshire or Barton St Mary in Sussex — or

ABOVE **Ragdale's living room provides an unpretentious, comfortable space, marred only by the rather unfortunate display of crossed golf-clubs over the fireplace — a sort of suburban equivalent of the arms and armour found in a medieval great hall.**

Voysey houses like Moorcrag on Lake Windermere (1898–9) and the architect's own Hertfordshire home, the Orchard (1899). What makes the comparisons the more remarkable is that all four of these houses postdate Ragdale, which was completed in about 1898. Far from slavishly copying turn-of-the-century English Arts and Crafts – something he is occasionally accused of – Shaw developed his style in parallel with those of the English architects he admired.

By and large, the interiors of Ragdale were as plain and self-effacing as the exterior. The front entrance, offset to one side of the porch, opened onto one end of a long transverse hall. A small staircase was tucked away on the right, and beyond it lay the kitchen, pantry, servants' hall, and other domestic offices. To the left, the hall led past a big dining room and into an even bigger living room which opened onto another porch at the rear of the house. The *Architectural Review*, in its generally laudatory account of Ragdale, was rather snooty about this layout. Its critic approved of the concealed stairs as "a step in the right direction, for we yet fail to see why the means of getting to bedrooms in a small house should be made monumental and the chief factor of the interior." But the critic was less enthusiastic about the hall:

"It might not be acceptable to some people to enter a hall that is somewhat of a corridor and pass the entrance to the dining-room, and, in fact, look into it through openings before reaching the living room, but in planning an American country house there are many men of many minds." (However, he did go on to admit that "all the rooms are worth looking into.")

Like many of the Lake Forest houses that Shaw designed, Ragdale was more of a weekend and summer retreat than a permanent residence. The family lived mostly in Chicago, but in early spring and late autumn they moved up to Ragdale for extended holidays. Shaw himself was a shy and retiring character, who suffered bouts of crippling indigestion at the thought of making a public speech or even attending a society party. He seems to have been at his most contented when he was out at his country home pursuing the country life – building a sleeping porch onto the side of the house, laying paths, working on the stables and outbuildings he had constructed in the grounds, or designing sets and lighting for open-air amateur dramatics. These were their happiest times, his wife later recalled – these and "the Harvest Moon Bonfires in the Ragdale Meadow, and the cider-making every autumn in the Ragdale orchard."

RIGHT This view of the south-east corner of the living room shows how Shaw designed it to be a light, airy, and above all simple space. Shaw was innovative in his development of an American style of domestic architecture that not only paralleled but pre-dated the projects of many of his British contemporaries.

DAS ENGLISCHE HAUS

Hermann Muthesius and the Arts and Crafts house

Early in 1897 Hermann Muthesius, a German architect and writer who had just been sent as an attaché to the German embassy in London, told the Grand Duke of Saxe-Weimar that he had ambitious plans for his time in England. "I am hoping in the near future," he wrote, "to find time for a project that is dear to my heart, namely, a thorough investigation and exposition of the English house." The result was *Das englische Haus*, a monumental three-volume exploration of English domestic architecture. Published in Berlin in 1904–5, shortly after Muthesius's return from his tour of duty in London, it dealt with the history of the house (which, as the author realized, "is also the history of a culture"), before going on to tackle its main

theme – developments in domestic building and interior design since the 1860s.

Because it was written by an outsider looking in on English culture, *Das englische Haus* is full of the sort of trivial yet fascinating details that a native writer would probably ignore. Inevitably there are sweeping, but nevertheless sometimes uncomfortably accurate, generalizations: the English "like beamed ceilings in their halls," for example, and are "less sociable by nature than the Germans." Less perceptively, Muthesius declared that the English gentleman rarely smoked and didn't drink, and that alcoholism was thus an exclusively lower-class problem. (One wonders just who was on the German embassy's social list.) He criticized English food as monotonous,

ABOVE **Richard Norman Shaw's own perspective drawing of his designs for Adcote, Shropshire (1875). Muthesius approved of Shaw's work, but declared himself slightly suspicious of the architect's inability "to break away from the romantic magic that the old English manor-houses hold for modern man."**

ABOVE **Hermann Muthesius was an enthusiastic propagandist for the Arts and Crafts movement, and his writings did a great deal to popularize design reform in Germany.**

BELOW **The dining room of I Palace Green, Kensington, decorated by William Morris with a frieze executed by Edward Burne-Jones and Walter Crane. "A document in the history of interior decoration," said Muthesius.**

admired the trend towards plainness in English furniture, and applauded the English habit of placing the bath and the toilet in separate rooms. The usual practice in Germany was to combine the two; this not only made the bathroom smelly but also prevented access to the toilet whenever anyone was taking a bath, "which might have awkward and inconvenient consequences."

But one of the most remarkable things about *Das englische Haus* is the extent to which Muthesius bought into the Arts and Crafts ideal. As far as he was concerned, Ruskin and Morris were the prophets of the new order. Philip Webb embodied "the best elements of English artistic sensibility in their purest form," and was thus "a classic representative of English good taste." Richard Norman Shaw was "the first of the modern architects" because he was "the first in the history of nineteenth-century architecture to show …freedom from the trammels of style." Among the work by designers of the post-Morris generation, Lethaby's houses were all "masterpieces"; Mackintosh (a personal friend of Muthesius) was the most outstanding younger architect of the day, while the houses designed by Lutyens were said to be "as convincing in their workmanlike efficiency as in their intimate, pleasing appearance and are undoubtedly among the best being built in England today."

Muthesius fell in love not only with the products of the Arts and Crafts movement, but also with the Morrisite anti-urbanism that helped to define the movement. He was not particularly interested in the improved housing being built for the working classes of the period, and especially not in the petit-bourgeois suburbs, with their "wretched, absolutely uniform small houses." The real attraction for Muthesius was to be found in the homes of the moneyed middle classes. He defined the type of house that most interested him as lying "…in the midst of flower-gardens, facing far away from the street, looking on to broad green lawns which radiate the energy and peace of nature; the house lies long and low, a shelter and a refuge rather than an essay in pomp and architectonic virtuosity; it lies hidden somewhere in the green countryside removed from any centre of culture… ."

At the same time, Muthesius was keenly aware of the tension at the heart of the Arts and Crafts movement. The curse of Arts and Crafts furniture, he wrote, was its idealistic emphasis on traditional methods of construction and its lack of economic viability — a lament that was echoed by almost every twentieth-century adherent: "We look for modern art, that is, for pieces that fully meet our modern requirements, and we find roughly jointed kitchen cupboards for which we are expected to pay as many pounds sterling as they are worth in thalers." Was it any wonder, he asked, that the public was scornful of such displays?

The extent to which Muthesius helped to spread Arts and Crafts ideas on his return to Germany is difficult to measure. The work and thinking of architects like Henry van de Velde remained much truer to Morris's anti-industrial vision. (Indeed, in 1914, van de Velde engaged in a celebrated public dispute with Muthesius in which each man championed his own view of the proper direction to be taken by modern design.) By contrast, although he approved and tirelessly promoted the architecture of the English movement, Muthesius was exasperated by its insistence on expensive, handmade artefacts. As far as he was concerned, creativity and the machine were not mutually exclusive. He felt that the only way to develop an economically viable national style was through the union of art and industry. And in this belief, tomorrow belonged to him.

HAUS OLBRICH

Joseph Maria Olbrich, 1901

The notion of a community of artist-craftsmen was dear to the heart of the Arts and Crafts movement. An entire settlement making beautiful things in beautiful surroundings seemed a natural consequence of Morris's ideas, a step along the way to the whole-sale reform of society. It appeared in various guises in late-Victorian and Edwardian England, from the Queen Anne Revival suburb of Bedford Park, west London, to C. R. Ashbee's 150-strong Guild of Handicrafts, which decamped from London to Chipping Campden in the Cotswolds in 1902.

Nor was it only in Britain that such communities were established. In 1899 Ernst Ludwig, Grand Duke of Hesse, invited seven young designers to form an artists' colony at Darmstadt. (A fan of the English Arts and Crafts movement, the Grand Duke had previously brought over C. R. Ashbee and M. H. Baillie Scott to decorate several of his wife's reception rooms at the Neue Palais.) The seven designers were: sculptors Rudolf Bosselt and Ludwig Habich, painters Hans Christiansen and Peter Behrens, interior designer Patriz Huber, decorative painter Paul Bürck, and architect

BELOW **Haus Olbrich at Matildenhöhe in Darmstadt, designed by Joseph Maria Olbrich in 1901, was both a home and an exhibition space for the display of his work. "What is the use of a beautiful street with beautiful houses,"** he asked, **"if the chairs inside them are not beautiful, or if the plates are not beautiful?"**

ABOVE **The architect Olbrich, seen here in his thirties, was invited to become part of a new artist's colony at Darmstadt by Ernst Ludwig, Grand Duke of Hesse, who took a keen interest in fostering Hessian arts and crafts. Although he was still young, Olbrich had already made an impact with his innovative designs, most notably the Secession Building in Vienna.**

RIGHT **Haus Olbrich was built on a prime site at Matildenhöhe, next door to the communal studios in Ernst Ludwig Haus, which Olbrich also designed. As the only trained architect among the seven designers who founded the colony, Olbrich was responsible for most of the buildings on the site.**

Joseph Maria Olbrich. After combining their talents in the so-called "Darmstadt Room," which won a gold medal at the Paris Exhibition of 1900, they began work on a show of their own, *Ein Dokument deutscher Kunst*, to be held amongst their new homes on the Matildenhöhe, a hill to the east of Darmstadt city centre which the Grand Duke had set aside for the colony. In fact, the exhibition was to be the group's new homes. There were galleries, pavilions, shops, a restaurant, and a monumental building containing artists' studios, which was called the Ernst Ludwig Haus in honour of the Grand Duke. But the focus of *Ein Dokument* was domestic design, and the artists' own houses doubled as display spaces open to the public. Matildenhöhe offered wealthy Germans a complete lifestyle permeated by Art with a capital

A, a continental European version of the House Beautiful popularized in Britain by Whistler, Wilde, and the Aesthetic Movement.

As the only professional architect in the group, Joseph Maria Olbrich (1867–1908) was responsible for designing most of the buildings on the site, including six of the seven houses built for his fellow group members. (Peter Behrens, who designed Haus Behrens, was later to become one of the founding fathers of the modern movement; however, at this period he was still primarily a graphic artist.) Although only thirty-three, Olbrich already had a considerable reputation. He had just caused a storm with his Secession Building on Friedrichstrasse in Vienna, known as "the Golden Cabbage" for its bizarre, leafy golden dome. Olbrich's work at Matildenhöhe, while less

OPPOSITE **The entrance to the house is reached via a short flight of steps up to this open porch, which is recessed into one corner of the building. The furnishings and decoration are a mixture of sinuous Art Nouveau and chunky Craftsman-like wooden furniture.**

dramatic than this earlier design, is more romantic, although its underlying assumption that the artist is above the common herd is mildly distasteful today. To Olbrich, the Ernst Ludwig Haus was "a temple, with work as the holy service," and the artists' own homes "a peaceful place, to which, after a hard day's work, [they] will come down from the temple of diligence to mix with the people."

Olbrich's own house stood on a triangular site on the Matildenhöhe next door to the Ernst Ludwig Haus. (It still does, although along with most of the other buildings, it was badly damaged during the Second World War.) It is constructed on three storeys over a basement and, externally at least, conjures up images of the traditional German rural vernacular. In Olbrich's time a short flight of

steps led to an open piazza, which contained a mixture of sturdy wooden furniture, Art Nouveau metalwork, and stencilled wall decoration. From here, the front door opened into a small *Vorraum* or entrance lobby, with a staircase at the far end. The dominant feature of the house was a large double-height *Halle*, inspired by the English living hall. The walls of the *Halle* were dark green, and the predominant colour of the geometrical-patterned carpet was a warm lilac. Pride of place went to a striking, angular white fireplace framed in bronze-green oak, with a copper canopy, which looked like a reinterpretation of a Moorish kiosk. But the weirdest feature of the room was a piano on a closed platform at first-floor level, entirely hidden from the sight of anyone below. The British magazine *The Studio*, reviewing the house in 1902, was much taken with this feature, noting that listeners would "hear the pure and beautiful sounds come floating down from above" without being distracted by "the technical side of the playing."

A small studio and a dining room filled the rest of the ground floor; the latter had white walls ornamented in gold, and plain cherrywood furniture. On the floor above were a further living room, Olbrich's bedroom, and a blue guest room. The upper floor contained servants' quarters, children's rooms, and two more display areas, the Green Room and the Red Room.

The Matildenhöhe experiment ended in failure. The 1901 exhibition was a financial disaster, and personal rivalries sprang up among the Seven. As the oldest member of the group, Olbrich assumed the mantle of leader and virtual artistic director — something that irritated the other artists. In the summer of 1902, Bürck, Christiansen, and Huber left the colony (Huber killed himself in Berlin that September); the next year they were followed by Behrens and Bosselt. Olbrich continued to work for the Grand Duke, and his reputation as an architect spread throughout Europe. But in 1908 Olbrich's glittering career was cut short when he became ill with leukemia. He died that August, aged just forty.

LEFT **The strong vertical emphasis in the lines of Olbrich's bedroom suggest a rather urban sophistication that belies the rural rusticity of the building's exterior. Contemporaries were not sure what to make of the style, criticizing it for being "too stiff, too straight, too linear."**

HVITTRÄSK

Herman Gesellius, Armas Lindgren, and Eliel Saarinen, 1902

Hvitträsk, a collection of studios and living quarters on the steeply sloping shores of Lake Vitträsk in Finland, was a venture in communal living on the part of three successful young architects. Herman Gesellius (1874–1916), Armas Lindgren (1874–1929), and Eliel Saarinen (1873–1950) were partners in GLS, the most talked-about architectural firm in Finland. They had established the practice while still students in 1896, and two years later won a competition to design Finland's pavilion at the 1900 World's Fair in Paris. This led to a string of commissions, from offices to country villas.

Early in 1901 the firm was approached by a wealthy music-shop proprietor, Robert Emil Westerlund, who wanted a residence on Lake Vitträsk, about twenty miles from Helsinki. Hvittorp, as the new house was called, was well suited to its remote and romantic setting, with a massive round tower breaking out from the main block, and a bewildering collection of balconies, loggias, verandahs, and various other projections.

It was while they were working on their designs for Hvittorp that Gesellius, Lindgren, and Saarinen conceived the idea of building themselves a sanctuary far removed from their existing office, which was on Länsi-Henrikintaku in Helsinki. Late in 1901 they bought a plot of land a mile or so from Hvittorp, and early the following year started work on a home of their own – Hvitträsk.

One can see in this decision echoes of the English Arts and Crafts movement's preoccupation with unspoilt countryside and its desire to escape from urban life. And the three partners were certainly well aware of cultural trends beyond Finland: they subscribed to the British magazines *The Studio* and *The Builder*, and some of their early buildings make obvious references to the work of Voysey and M. H. Baillie Scott. But architecture in turn-of-the-century Finland was much more of an overtly political act than it ever was in England. After six hundred years of Swedish rule, the country had been conquered by Russia in 1809. Successive czars allowed Finland a greater degree of

RIGHT A tiled stove in the corner of the vaulted dining room. The swirling Celtic designs on the wall above the stove – designs that are echoed on the ceiling and around the windows – reflect Saarinen's fascination with ancient Finnish motifs, a fascination that was characteristic of National Romanticism.

autonomy than other outposts of the Russian empire, with the result that the nineteenth century saw the steady growth of a national consciousness. But in 1899 Czar Nicholas II began a deliberate process of Russification, and Finns reacted by reaffirming their cultural identity in literature, the visual arts, and architecture, through what became known as National Romanticism, a movement that consciously celebrated Finnish traditions. The success of GLS's design for the World's Fair pavilion in Paris was in large part due to its sensitive reinterpretation of native architectural forms.

Hvitträsk operated within this nationalistic context. The idea of a house in such a wild setting drew on the mystical reverence for nature expressed in the *Kalevala*, the great epic poem of Finnish literature. The complex itself consisted of two self-contained wings connected by a single-storey studio section, with a separate annex on the other side of a central courtyard. The lower walls were partly plastered, partly faced with granite – seen as the most Finnish of building materials – and the upper walls were of unfaced and untreated log, another familiar motif in Finnish vernacular architecture. The roofs were pantiled, the chimneys plastered. The overall effect of this mix of materials and of the changing levels, from the long, low central studio to the massive square tower topped with a spire in the angle of the north wing, is undeniably both "National" and Romantic.

The interior planning and decoration borrowed ideas from both home-grown tradition and broader contemporary views on domestic design. For example, the two-storey-high living hall in the south wing, which Saarinen occupied, owed a great deal to Domestic Revival architecture in Britain (and especially to the writings of M. H. Baillie Scott). So did the general emphasis on high standards of craftsmanship, the sheer variety of materials — copper, brass, wrought iron, wood, plaster, brick, and textiles — and the muted, natural-looking colour scheme. Other features, such as the log-effect cladding of the upper walls of the living hall and the massive cylindrical stove, were Finnish through and through.

Architecturally Hvitträsk was a resounding success. As an experiment in communal living, it was a disaster. When work started on the building early in 1902, Lindgren and Saarinen had both recently got married. Gesellius was still single, and the design included a bachelor apartment for him in the annex, with Lindgren and his wife Irene occupying the north wing of the main block, and Saarinen and his wife Mathilda in the south wing. But even as the walls of Hvitträsk were going up, Saarinen's marriage was breaking down. After miscarrying in 1901, Mathilda spent the summer of 1902 abroad; soon afterwards, she seems to have begun an affair with Gesellius.

"What else can you expect, for Heaven's sake?" said the architect Jarl Eklund, who also lived at Hvitträsk in the 1900s. "Saarinen did nothing but sit and draw… I remember Matti sweeping along the street in front of the office in a gorgeous dress… and Gesellius arriving on a galloping white charger with a horse blanket of blue silk! What happened was inevitable. It should have been obvious to the biggest fool."

ABOVE **A contemporary view of the living hall in Saarinen's south wing, which was occupied by the architect and his second wife, Loja Gesellius. Loja's brother Herman lived in the north wing with Saarinen's ex-wife Mathilda, who was not on speaking terms with Loja. No wonder Armas Lindgren fled the communal complex!**

Whether or not it was obvious to Saarinen isn't clear. Stained glass in the south-wing dining room, designed by Olga Gummerus-Ehrström at about this time, shows a seventeenth-century maiden sitting uneasily between two admiring suitors, with Hvitträsk in the background: the three figures are clearly recognizable as Saarinen, Matti, and Gesellius. The Saarinens were divorced in January 1904, and on 6 March Gesellius and Matti were married. To complicate things further, Saarinen had fallen in love with Gesellius's sister Loja, and the pair were married on the same day.

Lindgren found it all too much, and he and Irene left Hvitträsk. Gesellius and Matti moved into the north wing, and the apartment across the courtyard was occupied by a succession of architect and artist friends, including Eklund, who

was married to another Gesellius sister. Gesellius and Saarinen remained friends. Their wives didn't. These personal tensions, coupled with growing artistic differences, eventually led to the end of the firm. Lindgren left in 1905 to pursue a career in teaching; the Gesellius–Saarinen partnership was dissolved the following year.

Although it began as a joint venture, Hvitträsk has come to be seen as Saarinen's house. This is partly because the Lindgren–Gesellius wing was devastated by a fire in 1922, but mostly because of Saarinen's subsequent fame as a designer, teacher, and planner, both in Finland and in the United States. He left his homeland in 1923, returning to spend his summers at Hvitträsk until 1949, the year before his death. The house now belongs to the Finnish government, and is open to the public.

A Place in the Country

In 1910 the magazine *Country Life* published a book called *Small Country Houses of Today*, a survey of forty-eight houses. Six were recent remodellings of old buildings, but the rest were virtually brand new, with the exception of Philip Webb's Red House, which was included because "no survey of modern domestic architecture can be complete without some reference to that notable and epoch-making work." The compiler and author of all but ten of the reviews was Lawrence Weaver, *Country Life*'s new architectural editor, and the book arose out of an influential series of articles he had begun the previous year. Weaver's aim was to show his largely middle-class readers that if they were thinking of building a new house in the country, there were plenty of architecturally interesting alternatives to the ugly bourgeois villa. Wherever possible, the examples he chose were priced, giving prospective buyers an idea of what they might expect for their money. They ranged from a "cottage" in Gerrard's Cross at £720 ($1,150) (with accommodation for just the family and a single servant), to Old Pound House, Wimbledon, a ten-bedroomed Wrenaissance affair built in 1903 at a cost of £5,080 ($8,000).

Stylistically, the buildings were a motley bunch, a reflection of the eclecticism of domestic architecture in Edwardian England. There was a smattering of Wrenaissance, of which the Old Pound House was the grandest example, and some self-conscious essays in the Tudor taste, all half-timbering, high chimneys, and jettied upper storeys.

BELOW **To Lawrence Weaver, who in 1910 surveyed the state of small country house design, a modernist experiment like Edgar Wood's Upmeads in Staffordshire (1908) was disturbingly un-English. "Unusual to the point of oddness," was Weaver's verdict.**

There was Kentish vernacular with sweeping roofs, tile-hanging, and weatherboarding, and a single, glorious precursor of the Modern movement — the Mancunian architect Edgar Wood's flat-roofed Upmeads in Staffordshire. But Upmeads excepted, all the examples in *Small Country Houses* were rooted in a romantic rural past, bearing out Weaver's dictum that "buildings, in suburbs and elsewhere, will fail of their appeal as homes, unless the imagination can relate them credibly with the houses of past days."

The collection included work by most of the big names of the Arts and Crafts movement. Some wear better than others: W. R. Lethaby's contribution, for example, a Jacobethan house on the outskirts of Birmingham, already seems a little too stiffly Victorian in comparison with the sweeping asymmetrical roofline of Voysey's Homestead at Frinton-on-Sea; a little too self-conscious beside Alfred Powell's Long Copse, a beautiful thatched *cottage orné* in Surrey. The two houses in Weaver's book that most successfully synthesize cultural references to the rural past with a new, more modern aesthetic were both the homes of Arts and Crafts designers. Ernest Barnsley's Upper Dorval and Ernest Gimson's nameless house, both at Sapperton in the Cotswolds, transcend historicism. Each looks back to the past and forward to a better life.

Small Country Houses of Today shows the strength of the dream that the England of sleepy unspoilt villages and leafy lanes could be restored, a quiet confidence that Utopia was on the doorstep, if we only had the reverence for decent things — and the money — to let it in. Yet even in 1910, there were signs that the English Arts and Crafts sensibility was beginning to retreat into determined quaintness. The parade of interiors with their Sussex chairs and barley-twist gate-leg tables, their relentlessly beamed living rooms, their oak settles, and pine dressers, all were harbingers of the nightmares to come. When Weaver published a second collection of houses in 1920, the formula was starting to seem a little tired. The world had moved on.

HILLES

Detmar Blow, begun 1914

For an Arts and Crafts architect, Detmar Blow (1867–1939) had a perfect start. In 1888, a chance meeting with the ageing Ruskin in Abbeville Cathedral led him to throw up his formal architectural training for a more "honest" apprenticeship in a builder's yard. He became a socialist, joined the SPAB – where William Morris and Philip Webb took him under their wing – and continued to learn his trade the hard way, by working as Ernest Gimson's site foreman on Stoneywell Cottage (see page 122). With help from Webb, he finally began to carve out a flourishing practice for himself around 1900, designing a series of country houses that were sometimes quietly unassuming, sometimes innovative, but usually faithful to the local vernacular. In 1910 Blow, who was by now a successful designer with an aristocratic clientele, acquired an equally aristocratic wife when he married Winifred Tollemache, granddaughter of the 1st Lord Tollemache of Helmingham Hall in Suffolk. Four years later he began to build Hilles.

Professionally at least, Blow's contact with blue blood seems to have diluted his taste for the Arts and Crafts hard line. Like a number of his contemporaries, he moved towards a more formal – and more lucrative – neo-Georgian style from about 1910 onwards. Then in 1917 he made a decision that effectively ended his career as a creative artist. He took up an invitation to become agent to the 2nd Duke of Westminster, acting, according to Lutyens, as "a sort of bailiff and

BELOW **Hilles in Gloucestershire, the romantic, faintly Elizabethanate home of architect Detmar Blow. The photograph shows the original thatched roof, which was replaced with stone tiles after a fire in the 1940s.**

maître d'hôtel." In private, however, he retained his Ruskinian Romanticism – and if proof of this were needed, it is there at Hilles.

Like its architect, Hilles had a great start. The house perches on one of the most spectacular sites imaginable, a ledge of the Cotswold hills over-looking the Severn Valley westwards towards Wales, and with breathtaking views northwards to the Malvern Hills. Yet it accepts those views without revelling in them, as though they were a plain fact of life rather than a feature. Blow deliberately set the main axis at right angles to the views and disdained the use of big picture windows – just as a sixteenth-century builder, a little frightened of the power of the elements, might have done. He chose a golden-grey Cotswold stone and a soft, lyrically Elizabethan style. The house was originally roofed with Norfolk thatch, a cheap option, certainly, but a bizarre choice considering the windswept situation and Blow's sensitivity to local tradition: it was replaced with more tradi-tional stone tiles after a fire in the 1940s. The thatch excepted, the gables and bays of Hilles recall another fine Gloucestershire house – Stanway, a sixteenth- and seventeenth-century mansion that Blow worked on in *c.*1913. But there is no attempt at fakery. Hilles belongs to the twentieth century: its lines are too vertical, its roofs just a little too sloping, its interiors too urbane, to be anything else.

In Blow's day those interiors were nevertheless plain, comforting, and uncluttered. They were furnished with an typical mix of recent handmade pieces and older, mainly Georgian items which presumably came from Winifred's family (although Detmar could also trace his lineage back at least as far as the seventeenth century – a portrait said to be by Peter Lely of one of his ancestors, the composer John Blow, hung in the house). One bed was dressed with Morris & Co. cretonne, and another upstairs room boasted a Morris tapestry of Botticelli's *Primavera*. A narrow stone hall, draped with diagonally striped, linen block-printed curtains, led into the Long Room, the main living area, which was hung with Mortlake tapestries. On the other side was the whitewashed dining room, with pride of place over the fire given to an elaborate cast of James I's coat of arms – a proud acknowledgement of Winifred Blow's Tollemache ancestry; the original came from Dorfold Hall, an old Tollemache house in Cheshire.

"The object to be gained in furnishing a room," said Halsey Ricardo in a lecture to the Arts and Crafts Exhibition Society in the 1890s, "is to supply the just requirements of the occupants, to accentuate or further the character of the room, and to indicate the individual habits and tastes of the owner." The rooms at Hilles do all three: they declare the principles of their construction quietly but firmly, glorying in an idealized vision of the life of a country squire, and there is a hearty masculinity to them that cries out for dogs, wood smoke, and dirty boots. Only the external walls are of masonry: internal partitions on the ground floor are formed from oak, with elm boards used for the studwork on the floor above. However, Blow wasn't averse to taking the occasional shortcut – the fake panelling in one of the bedrooms was made up of sheets of plywood with lengths of moulding nailed to them, and then painted white. Morris would have turned in his grave. And in the best SPAB fashion, there was plenty of sensitive and blameless recycling. The Elizabethan oak screen that separates the stone entrance hall from the Long Room came from Seckford Hall in Suffolk. Blow, of course, would hardly have conspired in the dismantling of an old country house, but the screen had passed through several hands by the time he came across it. It fitted perfectly without needing any alter-ation. And the oak staircase was re-used from one of his own houses – Little Ridge in Wiltshire, an Elizabethanate manor he had designed for the haberdashery magnate Hugh Morrison in 1904.

When this short-lived creation was remodelled, the Morrisons donated the staircase to Hilles, along with the kitchen dresser.

Family life at Hilles partook of all the solid country virtues and high-minded daftness that one expects from an architect with Detmar Blow's principles and social aspirations. On the one hand, the house was always a functional living space rather than a showplace. "The hall is paved with stone, which does not fear the muddiest boots," wrote his friend Neville Lytton in the 1920s; "the long drawing room has a floor of raw elm, which also cannot be injured by large boots with nails in the soles." One can almost see those spaniels. The other side of the rural idyll involved communal folk-singing after breakfast and country dancing in the evenings, with the whole household — servants included — being encouraged to join in. There was no nursery and the little Blows were never disciplined, with the result that there was "monstrous anarchy," according to Lytton. And, while the notion of doing without domestic staff was incomprehensible, even to someone with Blow's left-wing views, the segregation of servants and family was held to be socially divisive. So everyone ate together in the kitchen, an idea that was advanced and yet harked back to the great hall of the Middle Ages — until the embarrassed silences and awkward conversation eventually led the architect to abandon the idea, and he and his wife fled to the dining room.

Although the Blows had moved into Hilles by the 1920s, the architect never finished his house, and the last years of his life were clouded with disappointment. In 1930 the Duke of Westminster abruptly dispensed with his services. Blow had a breakdown and retired to Gloucestershire, dying in 1939. The following year Christopher Hussey wrote about Hilles for *Country Life*; his conclusion sums up its enduring appeal:

> Peace, quiet, happiness seem now all too truly to belong to a past age. Detmar Blow knew how to compound these precious elements. Here, looking towards the sunset, we may well envy the wisdom that led him to discovering for himself that the philosopher's stone which changes time itself to gold is, in reality, the stone, the wood, the wax, lying nearest to hand when it is moulded with simplicity of heart.

OWLPEN MANOR

Norman Jewson, restored 1925–6

A reverence for the past lay at the heart of the English Arts and Crafts movement. It drew its inspiration, its working methods, and its design vocabulary from the country masons and carpenters of the sixteenth, seventeenth, and eighteenth centuries. And not surprisingly, some architects and designers took this love affair with pre-industrial rural society beyond the borrowing of motifs and building techniques from ancient manor houses and picturesque farmsteads. They wanted to live in the real thing. Not so good for business, perhaps (although the twentieth century now has a long and not particularly honourable tradition of architects whose passion for modern design doesn't extend to their own homes), but a logical extension of the period's craving for authenticity. William Morris himself set the precedent in 1871, when he and Dante Gabriel Rossetti took a lease on Kelmscott, a rambling old manor in Oxfordshire. Among the others who followed suit was the likeable and much underrated Norman Jewson (1884–1975), who in 1925 bought and restored Owlpen Manor in Gloucestershire.

Jewson was a prolific architect with a highly respectable third-generation Arts and Crafts pedigree. After coming down from Cambridge he trained under Herbert Ibberson, who had been a pupil in the office of John Dando Sedding, along with Ernest Gimson and Ernest Barnsley. Sedding in turn had trained under G. E. Street; as had Morris, Philip Webb, and Richard Norman Shaw.

Jewson left Ibberson's office in 1907, setting off in a donkey and cart on a sketching tour of the Cotswolds, where Ibberson had suggested he should see the furniture workshop that Gimson and Barnsley were operating on Lord Bathurst's estate at Daneway. Jewson liked what he saw, persuaded Gimson to take him on as a pupil, and stayed with the workshop for twelve years (marrying Ernest Barnsley's daughter Mary in the meantime), before finally setting up his own office when Gimson died in 1919. He remained in the Cotswolds, where he restored old almshouses, repaired old barns, produced furniture, plaster-work, and church fittings, and designed dozens of cottages and country houses.

While working at Daneway and living in the Gimson–Barnsley community at nearby Sapperton, Jewson took the opportunity to explore the neighbourhood, eager to develop his technical knowledge of traditional Cotswold building techniques. One of these outings led him to the Gloucestershire village of Uley, ten miles west of his home. There, he came across Owlpen Manor, and immediately fell in love with this "very beautiful and romantically situated old house."

It isn't hard to see the attraction. Owlpen is one of the most delightful houses, in one of the most delightful settings, in England. It lies tucked away in a peaceful wooded valley, part of a little group of buildings that stand like a textbook of the best of English architecture: the manor's fifteenth-century barn, a Jacobean banqueting

LEFT **The interiors at Owlpen Manor boast a wealth of decorative details in metal, plaster, and wood. This pierced steel grille with a briar rose design, made by Alfred Bucknell in 1926, adorns the door linking the entrance hall to the service wing.**

RIGHT Owlpen Manor,
Gloucestershire, a
"very beautiful and
romantically situated
old house." When
Jewson bought Owlpen
in July 1925, the place
had been neglected for
nearly a century. The
bay window on the left
of the house had become
detached from the wall,
ivy was growing inside,
and the roof was about
to collapse.

house in the grounds, a Georgian mill, and, a few yards up the side of the valley, an early nineteenth-century church with an outstanding late-Victorian interior. The house itself is a mixture of stone and roughcast. Its gables and battlemented bays date partly from the mid-sixteenth century, when the wealthy Daunt family rebuilt the hall and great chamber on the site of an even earlier house, and partly from *c.*1616, when another Daunt added a new west wing. Other changes made over the years were mainly internal, and helped to engender the feeling of slow, organic development. They included an elegant panelled parlour dating from around 1720, and a remarkable set of painted wall-hangings with scenes from the story of Joseph, that were installed in the late seventeenth or early eighteenth century.

By the nineteenth century, following the marriage of the last of the Daunts, Mary, to an industrialist named Thomas Stoughton, Owlpen was abandoned, the Stoughtons having decided to build themselves a more fashionable Italianate mansion elsewhere on the estate. No longer a home, the house fell into a picturesque but structurally disastrous decline, becoming a favourite venue for antiquarians and romantics on day trips from Bath and Cheltenham. It was painted, photographed, and written up in *Country Life*, where it was described as "making its brave fight against consuming Time."

By the time Norman Jewson first saw Owlpen, it was clearly losing this brave fight. The only occupants were a caretaker who lived in the kitchen wing and showed tourists over the place, and a gardener who kept up the grounds. Jewson

ABOVE F. L. Griggs's 1930 etching of Owlpen turns its famous old yew tree walk into something wonderfully dark and sinister. Griggs also refuses to defer to pure romance in his depiction of the house itself, emphasizing its height to such an extent that, like the yews, the building towers up to the sky – remote, austere, threatening. During the War years the etching became an iconic image of a bygone England.

BELOW Today Owlpen is a repository for Sapperton group furniture and objects. This walnut and ebony writing cabinet was made around 1914 by Jewson's uncle-in-law Sidney Barnsley, while Ernest Gimson's traditional English working smock – embroidered by his wife Emily – is just visible in the mirror.

inspected the house, admiring the painted cloths and viewing the great chamber – said to be the room where Margaret of Anjou had slept during a stay in 1471, and (inevitably) still containing the very bed she had slept in. He also strolled in the garden, where groups of yews remained "just as they were in the time of Queen Anne." Saddened rather than charmed by the condition of the building, Jewson wrote that a hundred years of benign neglect had left Owlpen in such a state that "one of the main roof trusses had given way, the great stone bay window had become almost detached from the wall and huge roots of ivy had grown

right across some of the floors." Even so, he continued: "It seemed to me that such an exceptionally beautiful and interesting old house might still be saved." And he decided that he was the man to do it.

The problem was that Owlpen wasn't for sale. Its owner, Rose Trent-Stoughton, had no wish to sell, although at the same time she couldn't afford to repair it. However, when she died in 1924, her heir decided to sell off the bulk of the estate. It came up at auction in July 1925, and at last Jewson was able to buy the house, gardens, and outbuildings. It cost £3,200 (about $5,100).

For the next twelve months or so, he devoted his time – and a hefty sum of money – to mending Owlpen. Using traditional methods and local materials, and with help from local craftsmen (many of whom had trained under Ernest Gimson and Detmar Blow), Jewson stabilized the structure and repaired the stonework, roof timbers, and interiors. In all this he showed an uncommon sensitivity. There was no attempt to scrape away the layers of history, to falsify, or mythologize, but simply to show a respect for the basic integrity of the house, a desire to rescue something very precious before it was lost forever.

What makes this all the more heroic is that Jewson realized from the outset that he could never afford to make Owlpen his permanent home. He knew that once the work was done, he would have to give it up; and in November 1926, just sixteen months after he bought it, Owlpen was sold, at a loss, for £9,000 (about $14,400).

By no stretch of the imagination could Owlpen Manor be called an Arts and Crafts house. But it is something more: it is what so many English Arts and Crafts architects wanted their houses to be – many-layered and anchored to tradition. In 1930, F. L. Griggs produced a magnificent etching of Owlpen standing amidst its louring yews, with the inscription, "To my friend Norman Jewson, who, with one only purpose, and at his own cost and loss, possessed himself of the demesne of Owlpen when, for the first time in seven hundred years, it passed into alien hands, and with great care and skill saved this ancient house from ruin." Jewson made a successful career building and restoring in the Cotswolds. But if he had only done this, his reputation as one of the great names of the Arts and Crafts movement would be secure.

AMERICA THE BEAUTIFUL

California and the Arts and Crafts ideal in the United States

William Morris never visited the United States, although American agents were selling Morris & Co. products by the late 1870s, and the Firm's manager George Wardle travelled to Boston in 1883 to man a large stand at the Foreign Fair held that year. By the turn of the century *Ladies' Home Journal* could declare that "a William Morris craze has been developing, and it is a fad that we cannot push with too much vigour."

Morris himself may not have made the transatlantic crossing, but his ideals did. Several of the Arts and Crafts movement's leading exponents went to the United States to speak on modern design: Walter Crane lectured in Chicago in 1891, for example, as did C. R. Ashbee nine years later. And during trips to England, Americans imbibed not only the movement's design vocabulary but also its dream of rural communities of craftspeople working and living together. After a visit to the Kelmscott Press in 1893, the soap manufacturer Elbert Hubbard (1856–1915) was inspired to set up the Roycroft community in East Aurora, New York. Originally established in 1895 as a private press, Roycroft expanded until it was training and employing hundreds of local workers and making furniture, stained glass, and metalwork. The enterprise lasted over forty years before falling victim to the Great Depression.

Another American disciple of English Arts and Crafts was Ralph Radcliffe Whitehead (1854–1929), who first heard Ruskin's gospel while studying at Oxford. In 1902 he set up a similar handicrafts community to Hubbard's: the Byrdcliffe Colony, at Woodstock, also in New York. Unfortunately, like many of their English

RIGHT **The library at Frank Lloyd Wright's 1889 home in Oak Park, Chicago, part of the studio complex that he added to the house in 1898. The Arts and Crafts tradition in the United States was generally less hidebound by historicism than its British parent, and much more enthusiastic about forging a new, forward-looking architecture.**

LEFT The front entry and stairway of Bernard Maybeck's Grayoaks, in Marin County, California (1906). The extensive use of local timber in interiors, a favourite device of British Arts and Crafts designers in conveying a more natural, pre-industrial approach to decoration, was often employed even more effectively by their American counterparts.

timbers behind plaster. And in later buildings they committed the cardinal sin — as far as purists were concerned — of casing steel beams in more attractive timber. However, none of this detracts from their achievement, of which C. R. Ashbee, visiting the United States in 1909, wrote: "Here things were really alive…the 'Arts and Crafts' that all the others were screaming and hustling about, are here actually being produced."

To American designers, Arts and Crafts represented a new world, not an old one. One can see this philosophy in action in their enthusiastic adoption of the British fidelity to vernacular styles and local materials, using them to create new, regional architectures. This was perhaps nowhere more strikingly demonstrated than in California, where many architects adapted Arts and Crafts ideals with Spanish and Japanese motifs. The resulting houses suggest that it wasn't just a commitment to high standards of craftsmanship and unity of design that distinguished Arts and Crafts architects in America: their lasting achievement was their drive to make something that was new, yet imbued with a deep sense of place.

BELOW Modern homes by mail-order: the stone fireplace in this early twentieth-century bungalow was probably ordered from one of the many catalogues that specialized in Arts and Crafts products. A copy of Gustav Stickley's magazine *The Craftsman*, which did so much to popularize the movement in middle-class America, lies on the table.

counterparts, the workers at Byrdcliffe found harmonious living hard to achieve in practice; within a decade Whitehead's autocratic rule had driven most of them away.

The architectural response to Arts and Crafts in America was at once more diverse and, in many ways, more exciting than its progenitor on the other side of the Atlantic. In Britain, the towering presence of Morris was constantly drawing designers back to the past; they found it hard to confront the present or to build for a new future that accepted the realities of an industrialized society. While American architects acknowledged the moral arguments put forward by Ruskin and Morris, they were more pragmatic and less hidebound by dreams of a return to a pre-industrial utopia than their British counterparts. Pre-eminent among the work of these architects is the Gamble House (see page 82) in Pasadena, California, designed by Charles and Henry Greene, which compares with the finest British Arts and Crafts houses. Yet even this house shows a practical approach in its construction that would have been anathema to Morris. The Greenes sometimes used teak strips purely decoratively in the ceilings, although the real work was being done by pine

GRAYOAKS

Bernard Maybeck for J. H. Hopps, 1906

The highly individual architect Bernard Maybeck (1862–1957) is best known for two buildings. And they couldn't be more different. His masterpiece, and one of the great works of the American Arts and Crafts movement, is undoubtedly the First Church of Christ Scientist in Berkeley, California (1910), a strange and beautiful mix of High Victorian Gothic, Romanesque, and oriental, with Spanish pergolas and a cladding of cement-asbestos insulation panels on the outside and richly stencilled decoration on the inside. But his most famous work, in his lifetime at least, was the domed Corinthian rotunda of the Palace of Fine Arts created for the 1915 San Francisco Exposition, a piece of monumental neo-classicism that bears witness to Maybeck's early training at the Ecole des Beaux-Arts in Paris.

Maybeck's domestic buildings, most of them commissions in and around the Bay Area, tend to be less flamboyant than the Berkeley church, and more appealing than the Palace of Fine Arts. During the early 1900s he developed a Craftsman-like rustic chalet style, a rural architecture that promised sanctuary from the stiffly formal Queen Anne houses that were appearing in increasing numbers in San Francisco. The country houses designed by Maybeck often possess an attractive oddness, leaving one with the queer but not unpleasant feeling that the architect is having a private joke at our expense.

Grayoaks, also known as the J. H. Hopps House (1906), is a good example. Maybeck's client was a lumber magnate who owned a stretch of heavily wooded land in Marin County, an unspoiled and scenic landscape with easy rail access to San Francisco, fast becoming fashionable with wealthy industrialists who wanted to get away from the bustle of the city. It isn't known how or why Hopps settled on Maybeck to design his new country home, although the architect, who

ABOVE Trained at the Ecole des Beaux-Arts in Paris, Bernard Maybeck moved with equal ease between classical grandeur and rustic Arts and Crafts vernacular.

LEFT A view of Maybeck's Grayoaks in Marin County, California, designed for the timber baron J. H. Hopps in 1906, showing the block he added to the house in 1925. Maybeck's writings reveal an almost mystical approach to architecture: "There is something bigger and more worthwhile than the things we see about us," he wrote in 1923. "There is an undiscovered beauty, a divine excellence, just beyond us."

had started his practice in the early 1890s, already had an established local reputation for residential work, with well over twenty houses to his name.

Apart from the stone base and the brick chimneystacks, the dominant material used for both the façade and the interiors of Grayoaks was Maybeck's favourite redwood – a suitable choice for the home of a timber baron. The exterior walls of Hopps's new house were clad with overlapping redwood planks, giving a curious dappled texture that may have been intended to evoke Marin County vernacular (this form of cladding was more commonly used on barns) but which suggests an almost reptilian scaliness rather than quaint rural charm – an instance of Maybeck's ability to disturb our expectations, to remind us that a serpent dwells in Eden.

In spite of Hopps's considerable wealth, Grayoaks was never a grand house. Its size is exaggerated by the deeply overhanging chalet-style eaves – so deep, in fact, that although one of the chimneys projects out boldly from an exterior wall, it still pierces the eaves as it rises, to emerge, disconcertingly enough, well within the main roof. There are just four bedrooms on the upper storey, while the ground floor comprises a large living room with a dining room opening out of it on a slightly higher level, and an adjoining kitchen. The upstairs rooms have plain plaster walls, relying for their effect on the simple windows (and the spectacular views over the heavily wooded hills to be seen from them). The staircase hall, on the other hand, has a striking series of stepped windows, panelled in redwood below and plastered above. This device marks the transition from the lower to the upper floor, provides plenty of light, and – in a trick borrowed from Gothic Revival architects such as Pugin and George Gilbert Scott – expresses in visual terms the function of this part of the house as a means of ascent to the bedrooms on the upper storey.

The real heart of Grayoaks is, as it should be in any home, the living room, which is panelled, like much of the ground floor, in warm, welcoming redwood. The ceiling is criss-crossed with a matrix of massive timbers, suggesting solidity and permanence, all with the blade marks of the saw still visible on them. (As Maybeck told Charles Keeler nearly thirty years later, he hated "sham, veneers, and things done for sheer effect.

ABOVE The 1925 addition to Grayoaks consisted mainly of this large reception room (now used as the master bedroom). The Tudoresque chimneypiece is a slightly incongruous and very English feature, a half-conscious acknowledgment of Maybeck's debt to the British Arts and Crafts movement.

If the material used was wood, it should look like wood. . . .") The huge stone fireplace, with a redwood canopy corbelled out above it, offers another welcoming image of warmth. There is no sham here, no *faux* historicism – just a clean, stripped-down intimacy and a care for every detail, from the moulding of a corbel to the texture of a beam.

In 1925, nineteen years after completing the original Grayoaks design, Maybeck was called back to add a large reception room for entertaining. By this time his style, which had always been individual to the point of eccentricity, was becoming highly eclectic. The bizarre neo-classicism seen in his design for the Palace of Fine Arts was about to be repeated in the Packard Showroom on Van Ness Avenue, San Francisco, designed for the automobile dealer Earle C.

Anthony. And he was currently working on a Los Angeles home for Anthony, which threw together delicate Gothic motifs and the muscularity of a Spanish hill-fort.

By this time Maybeck had also seen many of his best early houses, including his own home and at least twelve other executed designs, destroyed in the fire that swept through Berkeley in 1923. As he entered his sixties, he had given up the direct supervision of every detail of construction that had characterized his earlier work, to concentrate on conceptual design, leaving the technicalities of finishes and decorative detailing to associates.

Even so, the 1925 addition to Grayoaks shows that Maybeck could still remain faithful to the Arts and Crafts' ideal. The new room was sited to one side of the original house and connected to it by a covered walkway. Roughcast rendering replaced the redwood scales of the main block, but the later work is stylistically linked by means of its shallow overhanging roofs and, internally, by the use of the same redwood panelling that features so prominently in the 1906 house. A solid Tudoresque stone chimneypiece and exposed roof timbers and trusses that declare their constructional technique show that, in domestic projects, at least, Maybeck's loyalties still lay with the English Arts and Crafts movement rather than with the florid beaux-arts classicism that was beginning to dominate his public buildings.

In 1923, the year of the Berkeley fire, Maybeck wrote that "there is something bigger and more worthwhile than the things we see about us... There is an undiscovered beauty, a divine excellence, just beyond us." In the course of his long career, he designed buildings that were both far grander than Grayoaks, and stranger. But with this house, the Radical Romantic came as close as any American architect to revealing that undiscovered beauty. For all its ambiguities, Grayoaks has a purity and a warmth that is more worthwhile than much of the domestic and civic architecture we see about us today.

RIGHT **As with so many of Maybeck's interiors, at Grayoaks warmth and comfortable domesticity are more important than grandeur and magnificence. The living room with its redwood boarding and ceiling of almost primitive, rough-hewn beams, has as its focus a massive and welcoming fireplace.**

GUSTAV STICKLEY

Founder of the Craftsman Workshops

A turn-of-the-century American who wanted to create an Arts and Crafts home needed to go no further than the Craftsman Workshops of Syracuse, New York. He could browse through the firm's mail-order catalogues, and within a few months he and his family would find themselves in a new Craftsman Workshops-designed house, eating at a Craftsman dining table and sitting on Craftsman chairs. In the evening, after the maid had drawn the Craftsman curtains and lit the Craftsman lamps, he might work on correspondence at his Craftsman desk, using his Craftsman blotter and inkwell, while his children played on the Craftsman rug and his wife leafed through her favourite journal, *The Craftsman*. And last thing at night, after he had prodded the dying embers of the fire with his Craftsman poker and stubbed out his cigar in his Craftsman ashtray, he and his wife could retire to their Craftsman bed, pausing on their way to look in on their children sleeping peacefully in their Craftsman cots.

The man behind the Craftsman Workshops was Gustav Stickley (1858–1942), who single-handedly introduced the Arts and Crafts movement

to middle-class America in the early 1900s. Born in Wisconsin, Stickley trained as a stonemason before going to work in his uncle's Massachusetts chair factory. By the 1890s he was a run-of-the-mill furniture maker with his own operation in New York, producing decent but undistinguished reproduction Chippendale – until a visit to Britain in 1898 brought him into contact with the new style. He returned home with a passion for Arts and Crafts: "I felt that the badly constructed, over-ornate, meaningless furniture that was turned out in such quantities by the factories was not only bad in itself," he wrote, "but that its presence in the homes of the people was an influence that led directly away from the sound qualities which make an honest man and a good citizen."

In 1899 Stickley founded United Crafts in Eastwood, New York; five years later this became the Craftsman Workshops. In the best tradition of Morris and Ruskin, the Workshops' output was underpinned by a belief that good design was a moral imperative: "Furniture as an educator," as one of Stickley's earliest advertisements read. The motto he chose for his new venture was *Als ik kan*,

ABOVE **Gustav Stickley was determined "to substitute the luxury of taste for the luxury of costliness; to teach that beauty does not imply elaboration or ornament; to employ only those forms and materials which make for simplicity, individuality and dignity of effect."**

RIGHT **Oak Craftsman bookcase.** Stickley held that the "the Craftsman idea makes for the development in this country of an art and architecture which shall express the spirit of the American people; for the creation of conditions which shall provide the best home environment for our children; for a form of industrial education which will enable men and women to earn their own living."

LEFT **A Craftsman settle of oak, with a single wide plank backrest.** The tenons and pegs are left visible, even prominent, showing Stickley's desire to provide American homes with furniture that declared its construction with pride.

Flemish for "As well as I can," which had been used back in 1857 by Morris in his very first embroidery, and recurred regularly as the legend "If I can" or more often, *Si je puis* in various Morris designs. The pieces produced in Stickley's workshops were a perfect expression of his desire "to do away with all needless ornamentation, returning to plain principles of construction and applying them to the making of simple, strong, comfortable furniture."

In 1901 Stickley began to publish a journal, *The Craftsman*, with the subtitle "In the Interests of Arts Allied to Labor." The first issue consisted of five articles on the life and work of William Morris; the second was largely given over to Ruskin. In February 1902 the first article on domestic architecture appeared, featuring a rather ordinary design for a house by the American architect

Henry W. Wilkerson, which was clearly derived from the work of M. H. Baillie Scott; and in May 1903 Stickley himself published a design, in collaboration with E. G. W. Dietrich, for the first of many houses to be called "The Craftsman House." It was unremarkable but pleasant enough, with walls and chimneys of irregular stonework, roughcast gables, and a mansard roof. A view of the main living hall showed how dependent Stickley was at this stage on English models, which were already coming to seem self-consciously quaint on the other side of the Atlantic. There was, for example, the inevitable beamed inglenook (a feature that subsequently reappeared in many Stickley houses) with a brick fireplace, copper hood, and built-in oak settle. This was just the sort of comfortable domestic scene that illustrated Stickley's belief that "The

No. 326
Arm Chair, Loose Seat
Cushion, Sheepskin - - - $15.00
Height of Back from Floor 37 in.
Height of Seat from Floor 18 in.
Size of Seat 19½ in. wide, 20½ in.
deep

No. 328
Dining Chair, Loose Seat
Cushion, Sheepskin - - - $10.00
Height of Back from Floor 37 in.
Height of Seat from Floor 18 in.
Size of Seat 19½ in. wide, 18 in. deep

No. 634
Dining Table
Height 30 in.
Thickness of Top 1⅛ in.
54 in. top to extend 10 ft. - $60.00
54 in. top to extend 12 ft. - 70.00
60 in. top to extend 12 ft. - 82.00

52

No. 817
Sideboard - - - - - $84.00
Height to Top from Floor 41 in.
Height to Top of Plate Rail 50 in.
Length 70 in.
Depth 25 in.
Top Drawer lined with Ooze Leather

No. 354½
Dining Chair, Hard Leather
Seat - - - - - - - $8.50
Height of Back from Floor 36 in.
Height of Seat from Floor 18 in.
Size of Seat 18 in. wide, 16 in. deep

No. 354½-A
Arm Chair, Hard Leather
Seat - - - - - - - $12.50
Height of Back from Floor 36 in.
Height of Seat from Floor 18 in.
Size of Seat 20 in. wide, 18 in. deep

53

LEFT Stickley produced illustrated catalogues every year – this one dates from 1910. The Workshops offered a complete range of household items, from chairs and tables to beds, fabrics, and lamps. Everything was available by mail order, direct from Stickley's New York factory.

BELOW Stickley jealously guarded the Craftsman reputation for quality, and ensured that his shop mark, a joiner's compass enclosing the motto *Als ik kan*, was stamped on every piece of Craftsman furniture.

word that is best loved in the language of every nation is 'home', for when a man's home is born out of his heart and developed through his labor and perfected through his sense of beauty, it is the very cornerstone of his life."

Over the next fifteen years, until it ceased publication in 1916, *The Craftsman* grew to become one of the most influential magazines of its kind. Although it promoted Stickley's own products, it also featured recent work by up-and-coming American architects and established European figures, including Frank Lloyd Wright, Irving Gill, M. H. Baillie Scott, and C. F. A. Voysey. There was often a surprising variety of material. The July 1916 issue, for example, contained poetry by Amy Lowell, Robert Frost, and Carl Sandburg, articles on Hopi architecture and gardens of the "western deserts," and designs for a range of buildings from complete Craftsman houses to "An All-Cement Chicken House."

Stickley also used *The Craftsman* to publish blueprints of furniture and detailed house plans. From quite early on, Stickley aimed for a total "look," providing perspectives of furnished in-teriors, wallpaper designs, curtains, and instructions for colour schemes. The extent to which he was personally involved in the design process isn't altogether clear. He was primarily a businessman and a propagandist, but the style that developed under his teams of designers certainly owed a great deal to Stickley's particular vision of what a small Arts and Crafts house should be. It is perhaps just as well that this vision was so strong, since his designers were not particularly distinguished – with the exception of the brilliant, but alcoholic architect Harvey Ellis (1852–1904), who was employed by Stickley in 1903–4 and who briefly introduced a much more sophisticated European curve reminiscent of Olbrich and van de Velde.

The Craftsman Workshops provided full working drawings of houses on request, and would even build them on site. The emphasis was on cheapness and convenience, and the houses were targeted at the suburban middle-class family. In the Craftsman House with Gambrel Roof and Wide Dormers, for example, prospective clients were advised to have a built-in table and benches in the kitchen: this would "save many steps in the early morning when business and school hours are pressing." The Craftsman Six-Room Cottage, a

LEFT AND BELOW
The sincerest form of flattery? The adjustable drop arm "Morris" chair shown below comes from the Craftsman Workshops, while this hexagonal oak table with its "wagon wheel" stretcher is the work of L. and J. G. Stickley, two of Gustav's brothers. "Some of the most persistent... imitators," Stickley wrote in 1910, "bear the same name as myself and what is called 'Stickley Furniture' is frequently, through misrepresentation on the part of salesmen and others, sold as Craftsman furniture or just the same thing."

straightforward three-up, three-down with shingle walls and a wide porch, was designed to appeal to "the housewife without a maid," while the Seven-Room Craftsman Cement Bungalow was planned for "a small family where one maid is to be kept." The furniture, metalwork, and fabrics that came out of the Craftsman Workshops were aimed at the same middle-class market, although their Arts and Crafts credentials were rather purer. The reasonably priced chairs, tables, desks, beds, and cabinets were usually of white oak, quarter-sawn to show the grain and fumed in ammonia cabinets to give a deep, mellow colour. Their structure was defiantly displayed, with exposed joints and pins, and they were rectilinear and simple in form. Everything was stamped in red with the Craftsman logo and Stickley's signature.

Like many Arts and Crafts designers in the United States – and unlike their British counterparts – Stickley made pragmatic use of assembly-line methods, so long as his high standards weren't compromised. However, he faced increasing competition from less talented imitators – including his own brothers, Leopold and George – who were happy to cut costs by using plywood where it didn't show and veneers where it did. In 1916 Stickley finally went bankrupt, unable to reconcile his principles with the commercial pressures of a mass market. The cover of one of the last issues of *The Craftsman* carried a poignant quotation from Chaucer: "The lyf so short, the craft so long to lerne."

THE GAMBLE HOUSE

Charles and Henry Greene for David Gamble, 1908–9

The Gamble House, in the city of Pasadena, southern California, is the most famous example of Arts and Crafts architecture in the United States. Its overhanging eaves cast their long shadow over book jackets, calendars, and post-cards; its rich, warm interiors welcome us into the pages of style magazines and scholarly textbooks; its furniture and fittings are still reproduced today.

What makes the Gamble House so special? Before we answer that, we need to explore the building's origins. In 1895 the forty-seven-year-old David Gamble retired from the family firm of Procter & Gamble, the Cincinnati soap empire founded by his father and William Procter fifty-

eight years previously. He and his wife Mary turned their eyes westwards to the open spaces and sunny skies of California – to Pasadena, where they already spent their winters, some ten miles north of Los Angeles. In June 1907 they bought one of six building plots on Westmoreland Place, a quiet private street with impressive views out over the San Gabriel mountains. Their neighbour, John Cole, had just begun to build his own house, designed by two local architects with a rising reputation: Charles Sumner Greene (1868–1957) and Henry Mather Greene (1870–1954).

The Greenes had been in practice in Pasadena since 1894. Born in Ohio and raised in St Louis, they studied architecture at the Massachusetts

BELOW **With its asymmetry, timber construction, and sprawling plan, the Gamble House appears to grow from the earth, giving the impression of being anchored to nature. Paradoxically, considering what a designerly and frenetic piece of architecture it is, the house achieves a sort of calm stasis.**

ABOVE **Charles Sumner Greene (left) and Henry Mather Greene (right) first encountered Japanese style at the World's Columbian Exposition in Chicago in 1893, where they saw the Ho-o-den, an exhibit that displayed traditional Japanese landscaping and architecture. The meeting was to prove a decisive influence on their work.**

Institute of Technology, having first attended the Manual Training School of Washington University, where woodwork and metalwork were an integral part of the curriculum. The latter school's philosophy, embodied in its watchword, "the cultured mind, the skilful hand," was ultimately a greater influence on the brothers than the conventional training they received at MIT. Even so, their early buildings, designed after they moved west to Pasadena in 1893, were undistinguished essays in American Wrenaissance, all pedimented porticos, columns, and Queen Anne detailing.

In the early 1900s, however, Greene & Greene began to evolve a more idiosyncratic personal style, unlike anything their wealthy Pasadena clients had ever seen, exposing structural features and turning them into decorative objects in their own right. It was described by enthusiastic contemporaries as a synthesis of Japanese and Scandinavian architecture, with a dash of the Tibetan frontier thrown in for good measure, but its underlying ethos came from somewhere rather closer to home – Gustav Stickley, to be precise. (The brothers subscribed to *The Craftsman*, and were specifying Craftsman furniture for a house within months of the magazine's appearance in 1901.) The Greenes' emphasis on the moral and aesthetic worth of honest construction went further back, of course, to the English Arts and Crafts architects of the 1880s and 1890s; it is probably no coincidence that their style began to develop in earnest soon after Charles Greene returned from his honeymoon in England in 1901.

But what made the brothers' mature work so striking was its reinterpretation of traditional Japanese forms. In the summer of 1893, they had visited the World's Columbian Exposition in Chicago, a celebration of the 400th anniversary of Columbus's discovery of America. With the other 27,539,000 visitors – almost half the total population of the United States – they saw the stuccoed white beaux-arts exhibition halls, the Aztec Temple, the "Streets of Cairo," and the pavilions from twenty-three foreign countries. And on a "Wooded Island" in the midst of the fair, they saw the Ho-o-den, a compound designed to show off Japanese landscaping and architecture from the twelfth, sixteenth, and eighteenth centuries.

The Greenes had apparently never seen traditional Japanese architecture before, and the stylized wooden post-and-lintel buildings – and the care that went into relating those buildings to their surroundings – must have made quite an impact. By the early 1900s they had rejected the historicism of their contemporaries in favour of a synthesis that drew on Arts and Crafts theory, and combined oriental building types and decorative details with those of other timber-based architectures, such as Swiss chalets and Norwegian cabins.

By the time Greene & Greene started to work out their designs for the Gamble House in the summer of 1907, their distinctive style was already fully developed. The contract drawings are dated 19 February 1908, and the building work was completed in January of the following year, one month ahead of schedule. The architects worked with another pair of brothers, John and Peter Hall, whom they had been using as their builders and furniture makers since 1906. But every detail, right down to the art glass in the windows and the mahogany-framed light fittings, was designed and supervised by the Greenes. So was much of the furniture, which was made in the Hall workshop and installed in the house between 1909 and 1911. There were exceptions: they ordered sturdy Craftsman furniture from Gustav Stickley for the Gambles' teenage sons, and David Gamble shipped in a roll-top desk and Morris chair from his Cincinnati office. But overall, the house and its contents are the Greenes' creation, from the piano in the living room and the inlaid black walnut furniture in the main bedroom, to the dining table and the stylized spreading branches of native oak that decorate the stained-glass entrance screen.

The Gamble House is big without being grandiose, and the way in which the rooms open into each other or break out into the grounds makes the interior spaces feel almost like the self-contained connecting pavilions of a Japanese villa. On the ground floor is a hallway which accesses David Gamble's study, the main staircase, and the living room on one side, and a service stair, the dining room, and kitchen on the other. Up above there are four main bedrooms, three of which have their own open-air sleeping-porches projecting beyond the walls, supported by massive timber posts or

BELOW Both the Gamble House itself and the elements within it declare their construction with a supreme confidence found in few other Arts and Crafts buildings, on either side of the Atlantic. Here, every joint, peg, and strap of the principal staircase is exposed and made part of the decorative scheme. The art glass that Charles Greene designed for the entrance doors can be seen in the background.

jettied out on shaped brackets. Like all of the structural wooden members, their hard edges were carefully planed and sanded, giving the building a muted and pliant quality. The external walls themselves are clad with redwood shingles, although the surfaces are so irregularly punctuated with windows, porches, and projecting bays, so softened with planting, so overshadowed – quite literally – by the overhanging eaves, that they assume a secondary importance. The overall effect is of an astonishing variety of advancing and receding planes and rising and falling levels.

Wood is the dominant motif in the interiors, making them dark and welcoming after the glare of the Californian sunshine. There is Burma teak, redwood, white and red cedar, Honduras mahogany, Oregon pine, and American white oak. And everywhere the building's apparently artless construction declares itself: in the metal straps and wooden wedges that hold timber elements together (one of many features borrowed from Japanese architecture); in the square wooden pegs that secure the curved oriental trusses of the living-room inglenook; in the elaborate jigsaw of interlocking timbers that make up the staircase. True, the Greenes were sometimes carried away with the idea of honest construction as decoration in a way that would have had English Arts and Crafts architects reaching for their Ruskin. They were also not above using wooden pegs to disguise the brass screws or bolts that really held a piece of furniture or a structural feature together. But just walk into the Gamble House and one can forgive them anything.

Which brings us back to that original question: what is it about the house that sets it on the same pedestal as, say, Webb's Red House? Partly, it is an accident of fate: in 1966 the Gamble family presented the house and its original furnishings to the City of Pasadena, and this very act of giving the public open access to an historic house (much rarer in America than in Britain) helped to turn it into an icon. But perhaps the answer really lies in the house itself: in the quality of care in which the tiniest detail receives as much attention as the greatest; in the sense of unity and harmony that comes from the Greene brothers' approach to total design; and in the tranquillity that derives finally from Japan, but which in their hands has been transformed into something unique to California.

ABOVE A detail of the rubbed-brick chimneypiece in David Gamble's office, at the point at which it meets one of the strapped and wedged beams that span the ceiling.

RIGHT Total design. Like much of the furniture in the house, the table and chairs in the dining room were commissioned by Greene & Greene, as was the hanging light fitting, the built-in sideboard of Honduras mahogany, and the art glass above it, which depicts a blossoming vine.

HOW THE WEST WAS WON

The American Arts and Crafts movement was far more active than its English counterpart in producing literature that extolled the virtues of honest construction and faith in good materials. The works of both Morris and Ruskin were best-sellers in the United States, and clubs and societies were formed to promote their ideas all over the country. In 1896, for example, Bernard Maybeck's friend and first client, Charles Keeler, formed the all-male Ruskin Club in Berkeley, with the purpose of exploring the practical implications of Ruskin's theories; two years later members' wives started its female counterpart, the Hillside. At the other end of the scale were the specialist magazines, of which Stickley's *The Craftsman* is best remembered today. Others included *The Philistine* (1895–1915), *The Bulletin of Arts & Crafts* (1911–12), *Arroyo Craftsman* (1909), and *The Bungalow Magazine* (1909–18), "An Illustrated Monthly Magazine Devoted Exclusively to Artistic Bungalow Homes." These journals were often a blend of practical advice and hard marketing, published by companies and craft communities to advertise their wares. They usually contained a mixture of plans and reviews, hints on home decoration, and inspirational articles, with a strong emphasis on domestic virtues and the sanctity of the home. The quality of the prose varied from passable to plain embarassing, as in "The Fireplace at Yule-tide," a leading article from *The Bungalow Magazine*'s Christmas 1912 issue:

> In this, the season of quiet evenings spent within the four walls of home, we are again reminded of the warm welcome which always awaits us when we turn to our cheery old friend, the fireplace… A gust of wind brings rain and sleet against the window panes, and we draw yet a little closer to the fire, which seems always beckoning – beckoning. Above it the wide mantel awaits the Christmas fringe of stockings, large and small, filled with the mysterious parcels so dear to the hearts of all of us; and the little red and yellow goblins which the children tell us are dwellers in the

LEFT A stone bungalow in Rochester, New York, *c.*1912. Built at a cost of around $3,500 and probably designed by the Pasadena firm of Arthur S. Heinemann, it started life the previous year as Plan 103 in Edward E. Sweet's *Bungalows*, an eighty-five page catalogue of plans and façades.

fireplace, keep vigil over all, sputtering in gleeful anticipation of the joys of Christmas morning. Verily, what is Christmas without the fireplace with its yule-log?

Inevitably, these little magazines tended to preach to the converted. But there was also a growing number of illustrated mass-market publications that began to appear at the end of the nineteenth century and reached a far wider audience, helped along by new print technology and an improving transcontinental rail network. The Philadelphia-based *Ladies' Home Journal* was first published in 1883, and Chicago's *House Beautiful* in 1896. *Architectural Record* appeared in 1891 and, following the successful launch of Britain's *Country Life* in 1897, *Country Life in America* arrived in 1901. None of these journals or their many lesser-known cousins specialized in the products of the Arts and Crafts movement, but they were all quite happy to feature Arts and Crafts homes and furnishings alongside the floral chintzes and beaux-arts mansions of the rich and famous. It was *Ladies' Home Journal*, for example, that published two influential Frank Lloyd Wright projects for Prairie houses in 1901, "A Home in a Prairie Town" and "A Small House with Lots of Room in It." *House Beautiful* regularly ran features with titles like "An Arts and Crafts House," "Bungalow Pottery," and "The Home of a Crafts-

man on the Pacific Coast." And *Country Life in America* reported on "English Cottage Types in America" and "Cotswold Influence in America."

But perhaps even more influential than the lifestyle magazines were the pattern books and catalogues that flooded the US market in the early 1900s, catering to the demand for low-cost homes. In catalogue after catalogue, enticing illustrations of shingled and weatherboarded bungalows with low-pitched overhanging roofs accompanied text promising that for just $1,000, $2,000, $3,000, you could have your very own three-bedroomed "house beautiful." All prospective home-owners had to do was send off $15, and in return they would receive sets of plans, complete lists of materials required, and detailed working drawings of every feature from mantels and window frames to built-in bookcases, spice drawers, and flour bins. For every one of these homes that was actually built – and they were built in huge numbers – there must have been a hundred couples who looked through the catalogues and dreamed of the day when they too could live in an Arts and Crafts house.

LEFT A view looking from the living room of the Rochester mail-order bungalow shown opposite. One of the more obvious results of the popularity of catalogue designs was that clones sprang up all over the country; the Rochester house, for example, has a twin in Pasadena.

ABOVE The staircase at Craftsman Farms in Morris Plains, New Jersey, built in 1910 by Gustav Stickley as the clubhouse at the centre of a proposed artistic community and design school. In spite of Stickley's tireless promotion of the Arts and Crafts ideal, he soon abandoned the scheme and turned the clubhouse into his family home. The picture shows Stickley's "S" monogram running up the stairway. The chairs come from his Craftsman Workshops.

HOLLYHOCK HOUSE

Frank Lloyd Wright for Aline Barnsdall, 1920–21

Hollyhock House, an exotic complex of blocks and terraces that rears up over Hollywood Boulevard like some strange temple, is one of Frank Lloyd Wright's (1869–1959) most engaging houses. And like all of his work, it is very much a personal creation.

But there was another powerful personality involved in the building of Hollyhock House – the heiress Aline Barnsdall (1882–1946), whom Wright referred to as his "most difficult client." The daughter of a Pittsburgh oil baron, Aline was kept under investigation by the FBI for almost twenty-seven years, which suggests that she must have done something right. And so she had. She was a rich radical with a healthy disdain for

convention – a socialist, an ardent pacifist, a birth-control campaigner, an unmarried mother by choice, and a champion of anti-establishment causes. It was her friendship with Emma Goldman, the anarchist agitator once described by J. Edgar Hoover as one of the most dangerous women in America, and her support for the imprisoned labour organizer Tom Mooney, who had been wrongly convicted of a terrorist bomb outrage in San Francisco in 1916, that led the FBI to open a file on her and not to close it until after her death.

As if she didn't have enough drama in her life, Aline was also deeply interested in the theatre, forming her own company and putting on a number of plays with varying degrees of success.

BELOW **Left unfinished when the client Aline Barnsdall lost patience with Frank Lloyd Wright and dismissed him, Hollyhock House in Los Angeles was partially completed in 1923 (as an independent commission) by Wright's assistant, Rudolph M. Schindler; his son, Lloyd Wright, carried out major renovations from 1946 to 1958.**

She also cherished plans for what she called "a permanent experimental theatre organization," the purpose of which was to be "the development of American talent in writing, acting, staging, and everything else that is a part of the creative theatre." Although she hadn't yet decided on a base for the project – Chicago, San Francisco, and Los Angeles were all mooted at one time or another – in 1915 or 1916 she approached Frank Lloyd Wright and asked him to design a complex to house it.

Wright's life at this point was in something of a muddle. The Prairie houses he had designed in the 1890s and 1900s, from the Winslow House in River Forest, Illinois (1894), to the Robie House in Chicago (1907–9), clearly reflected his Arts and Crafts roots. But his quest to develop an indigenous style that didn't rely on European traditions – itself a thoroughly Arts and Crafts notion, of course – was leading him to experiment with more avant-garde forms.

As Wright was beginning this search for new modes of expression, he suffered several crises in his private life. In 1910 he caused a scandal in Chicago society when he deserted his wife and six children for Mamah Borthwick Cheney, the wife of one of his clients. After travelling in Europe to escape the gossip, the couple settled in Wisconsin, where Wright devoted himself to building a new home, Taliesin; but in August 1914 a deranged servant set fire to the house, killing Mamah Cheney and six other members of the household.

Wright almost immediately began to pour his energy and a great deal of money into rebuilding Taliesin, and although he wasn't particularly short of work, Aline Barnsdall's major commission must have been welcome. The death of her father in February 1917 had made her a very wealthy woman, but the birth of her daughter Sugar Top three months later, combined with problems over her father's estate and her continuing indecision about exactly where the theatre was to be built, meant that little happened for several years. In the meantime, she paid Wright a $2,500 retainer and

RIGHT Hollyhock House takes its name from the rows of highly stylized hollyhocks that adorn its exterior. Wright later claimed that Aline Barnsdall had already decided that her favourite flower should play a major part in the decoration even before he began his designs, and simply asked him to render it "as Architecture how I might."

wrote him letters begging to see preliminary sketches, apparently without realizing she was talking to an architect for whom the relationship between structure and site was fundamental.

In June 1919 Aline finally bought Olive Hill, a 35-acre plot between Hollywood Boulevard and Sunset Boulevard in Los Angeles. By now her ideas had developed into something quite grand; a landscaped park with its own lake was to contain a 1,250-seat theatre; a cinema; an apartment block for actors, dancers, and musicians; a house for the director; and a row of shops on the edge of the site that would help to fund the whole enterprise. Wright was also to design two further houses, known as Residence A and Residence B. And on the highest point, like a Parthenon looking down on this Acropolis of the performing arts, there would be Hollyhock House – a home for his client and little Sugar Top.

The house takes its name from the flowers, stylized to the point of abstraction, that occur everywhere on the house as friezes and finials, on columns and on planters. "A bit sentimental," Wright later said, claiming that Aline pre-named her home and asked him to render her favourite flower "as Architecture how I might." But there is nothing remotely sentimental about either the building or its decoration. Its clean, hard angles

ABOVE **The fortress-like main entrance to the house: a pair of 300-lb concrete doors flanked by stark walls, with all the sentimentality of a fallout shelter.**

and tapering verticals evoke Mayan temples and pueblo dwellings. They suggest an indigenous architecture that acknowledges its debt to native American forms just as overtly as the British Houses of Parliament pay homage to the Gothic, or an Adam country house respects the classical remains of ancient Rome.

A long open loggia leads to the low entrance, a pair of 140-kg (300-lb) concrete doors flanked by stark walls with all the sentimentality of a fallout shelter. Once inside, the visitor is presented with a bewildering number of choices. On the left, steps lead up to the dining room and a colonnade which stretches along the north side of a central garden court; a little further on, across another loggia, a pergola on the south side of the court runs past guest rooms to Sugar Top's nursery in the south-east corner. And to the right, on the west side of the courtyard, are the main reception rooms – a music room, a library, and, between them, a big living room opening onto a rectangular ornamental pool.

The living room is the grandest space in the house. The sharp angularity of the exterior carries through into the Wright-designed furnishings (lost from the house, but recently replaced with reproductions) and the room's dominant feature, a monumental fireplace, the heart of which pushes out into the room and is surrounded by a small indoor pool, bringing together air, earth, fire, and water. A stylized overmantel panel depicts Aline Barnsdall as an enthroned Indian queen looking out over the deserts of southern California to the rocky tablelands beyond.

Sadly, Aline's "permanent experimental theatre organization" never saw the light of day: the project was halted in August 1921, with the first-floor interiors of Hollyhock House still incomplete. (They were finished two years later by Wright's assistant, Rudolf M. Schindler.) Wright later implied that the project foundered on artistic differences – just another case of a blinkered client blocking the creative genius of the architect. This was unfair. (When an interviewer asked her what style she was choosing for the Olive Hill complex, Aline simply replied, "Why not leave that all to the individual judgement of the architect?") The real reason for the scrappy ending to the affair was that by the time the project was finally given the green light, Wright had other things on his mind. He was spending long periods of time in Japan, immersed in the building of the Imperial Hotel in Tokyo. Aline grew increasingly impatient with the delays, the prevarications, and the detailed drawings that were promised but never arrived.

Costs spiralled upwards as the project management spiralled down into chaos. Wright fell out with Aline's business manager on site, calling him "a cross-eyed coyote" for presuming to interfere in the relationship between architect and client. Residence A, which was actually completed that July, cost $20,000, almost the budget for the main house. Aline Barnsdall refused either to put up any more money or to agree to further building until the house was finished, imposing a deadline of July 1921, when she would return from a trip to Europe. When Wright failed to comply, she simply pulled the plug. She presented Hollyhock House to the City of Los Angeles in 1927.

RIGHT **The living room in Aline Barnsdall's Hollyhock House. Most of the original furniture designed by Wright was lost from the house but has recently been replaced with modern reproductions.**

CASA DEL HERRERO

George Washington Smith for George F. Steedman, 1922

In an address given at Santa Fe, New Mexico, in 1880, General William T. Sherman dismissed the historic architecture of the American south-west, the white-walled Spanish missions and unadorned Indian pueblos, as unsophisticated and naive: "I hope that ten years hence there won't be an adobe house in the Territory. I want to see you... make them of brick with slanting roofs. Yankees don't like flat roofs."

This was the same General Sherman who burned Atlanta in 1864; presumably Yankees didn't much like colonial classicism, either. More

to the point, cultural difference spelled disaster to a diverse and disparate nation scarcely a century old. Enforcing the norm was everyone's patriotic duty. In architecture this meant the solid, stolid Anglo-American style prevalent in the "civilized" eastern states, one that drew heavily on the Gothic and classical traditions of Britain.

Yet in 1922, when an architect with the impeccably patriotic name of George Washington Smith (1876–1930) designed Casa del Herrero at Montecito on the Californian coast, about a hundred miles north of Los Angeles, he created

BELOW **The south front of Casa del Herrero, designed by the stockbroker-turned-painter-turned-architect George Washington Smith for George F. and Carrie Steedman. Casa del Herrero was a collaboration between Smith, the Steedmans, and their landscape architect Ralph Stevens.**

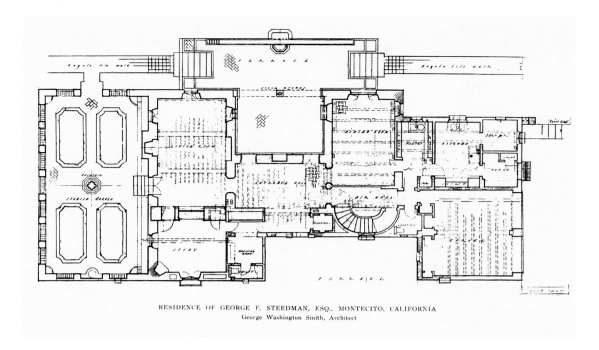

RESIDENCE OF GEORGE F. STEEDMAN, ESQ., MONTECITO, CALIFORNIA
George Washington Smith, Architect

RIGHT The floor plan of Casa del Herrero. The two projections to the south (facing upwards in this view) contain the living room on the left and the dining room on the right; they are separated by the entrance hall. Steedman's study lies behind the living room, which opens into a walled garden; the garage and service areas are to the right.

a house that looked for its inspiration to the eighteenth-century architectural traditions established by Spanish settlers in southern California. And everybody loved it. What had happened in the forty-two years since Sherman's breathtaking display of cultural imperialism?

What had happened was the Arts and Crafts movement, which worshipped the local vernacular – any local vernacular – and set its face against exactly the sort of homogeneous national architecture that Sherman advocated. The harsh realities of Spanish colonial oppression were forgotten, particularly in southern California, and the past was reinvented to offer a rosy Ruskinian picture of Franciscan friars and Indians working together to build their missions, using only local materials, primitive tools, and their own hands. The Mission Style, as it became known, also offered states like California a clear and distinctive cultural identity.

Mission Revival buildings began to appear in large numbers in California during the 1890s. Examples included A. C. Schweinfurth's Hacienda del Pozo de Verona at Pleasanton (1895–1910), a block-like fortress of a house built for Phoebe Hearst, mother of William Randolph Hearst. In the following decades Irving Gill produced a series of stark, almost cubistic buildings, notably his Luther Dodge House in Los Angeles (1914–16). Gustav Stickley's Craftsman furniture was sometimes known as "Mission," partly because it

faintly resembled eighteenth-century Spanish colonial work, but also because of Stickley's oft-repeated dictum that all pieces of furniture must fulfil a "mission of usefulness" – a conflation of themes that led to almost every piece of Arts and Crafts furniture in America being called Mission. When George Washington Smith arrived in California in 1915, the lofty ideals of the Mission Revival had been diluted somewhat, and its stylistic simplicity was giving way to the more grandiose Spanish Colonial Revival.

Smith was an interesting character. Born in East Liberty, Pennsylvania, in Centennial year and on Washington's birthday – hence his name – he trained briefly as an architect before becoming a stockbroker; by the time he was thirty-six he had made enough money to retire and take up a third career as a painter in Paris. He returned to America when war broke out, settling at Montecito, just outside Santa Barbara, where he built himself a studio-residence based on the Andalusian farmhouses he had seen on a trip to Spain in 1914.

The studio caused quite a stir, but as Smith later recalled rather ruefully, "People were not really [as] eager to buy my paintings, which I was laboring over, as they were to have a white-washed house like mine." Among those who beat a path to his door was George F. Steedman, a St Louis businessman with a passion for all things Spanish; the result was Casa del Herrero.

The house is compact, with most of the action taking place on the south front, where a dining room and good-sized living room project forward to either side of the entrance hall. From outside, however, these projections are effectively masked by a double-arched screen linking the two wings and forming an open loggia that looks onto a narrow terrace. Beyond this is a rectangular lawn, dominated by a pool in the shape of an eight-pointed star, and beyond that a narrow water channel, almost Moorish in conception, that cuts through shallow stone steps to continue the axial vista along a formal alley, which terminates in a little tiled garden room.

The distinction between exterior and interior is likewise blurred on the east front, where the beamed living room, packed to the brim with Steedman's Spanish antiques, opens out onto a walled patio paved with brick, decorated with Spanish tiles, and adorned with a low fountain in the centre. This also leads into an axial succession of gardens; both loggia and patio are crucial transitional areas between the house and its gardenscape, establishing a remarkable unity through a delicate progression from cool, rich interiors to sunny, flower-filled open spaces.

To help him furnish the house, Steedman commissioned Arthur Byne and Mildred Stapley, well-known dealers in antique Spanish artefacts and the authors of a string of books on the subject. Among the items they sold him were decorative ironwork, genuine and reproduction tiles, and a complete fifteenth-century painted ceiling, which found its way from the convent of San Francisco near Naranco to Casa del Herrero's entrance hall.

Steedman's eagerness for a "real" Spanish villa, along with the rich interior decoration, sets Casa del Herrero apart from the Arts and Crafts mainstream, even if that is where its roots ultimately lie: to doctrinaire Arts and Crafts designers, authenticity equalled fakery, and fakery equalled dishonesty – the cardinal architectural sin. But Smith's success in creating something that met his client's wishes, expressed a distinctive regional identity, paid homage to local tradition, and, most important of all, was a nice house to live in, more than makes up for the dishonesty.

THE GILLETTE RANCH

Wallace Neff for King C. Gillette, 1929

King Camp Gillette (1855–1932) was one of those colourful characters that the late nineteenth and early twentieth centuries seemed to throw up in abundance, both in Britain and in the United States. A brilliant entrepreneur and an immensely rich capitalist, he was filled with a zeal to build a fairer world based on principles of social equality; and he possessed a hold on reality that was tenuous, to say the least.

Born in Wisconsin, Gillette moved with his family to Chicago in the early 1860s, and later worked in a hardware store before becoming a travelling salesman. By the early 1890s he had developed an abiding, if eccentric, interest in the subject of social reform, believing that the answer to all society's problems lay in the formation of a

global corporation, the United Company, devoted to "Producing, Manufacturing, and Distributing the Necessities of Life" for everyone, everywhere in the world. As he wrote in *The Human Drift* (1894), the first of a series of polemical tracts promoting his new utopia, this would also involve a revolution in urban planning: "Under a perfect economical system of production and distribution, and a system combining the greatest elements of progress, there can be only one city on a continent, and possibly only one in the world."

Gillette therefore advocated the creation of Metropolis, a huge new city sixty miles long and thirty miles wide, which was to be situated beside Lake Ontario and would draw its electricity from Niagara Falls. The whole 60-million-strong population of America would live in this gigantic urban complex, in 24,000 identical tower blocks, each capable of housing 2,500 souls:

> In the construction of this city, durability of
> structure in every part is of first importance;
> and to this end steel has been used through-
> out its entire framework, and brick or terra-
> cotta is used as the material of greatest safety
> and durability, in all walls, ceilings, and floors,
> both the steel framework and the brick being
> afterward protected and covered from view by
> a facing of glazed tile or glass in every part of
> the structure, both inside and outside.

Gillette's Metropolis was to be organized on three covered levels. The lowest would contain pipes, wiring, and other services; the second would be devoted to an electric transport system connecting every apartment block; and the third would be:

> ...a bewildering scene of beauty in its artistic
> treatment. The floors, ceiling, and pillars of

LEFT **Innovator, entrepreneur, and inventor of the disposable razor blade, King C. Gillette also harboured ambitious plans to relocate the entire population of the United States to a metropolis of high-rise apartment blocks beside Niagara Falls. When it came to the planning of his own home, he opted for a more relaxed approach to living.**

porcelain tile, with their everchanging variety
in colors and designs, the artificial parks
topped above the upper platform with domes
of colored glass...[the] urns of flowers, and
beautiful works of art and statuary, would
make it an endless gallery of loveliness.

Gillette reckoned that this wholesale
reorganization of society would take a mere
twenty-five years to achieve. Perhaps not
surprisingly, his fellow-Americans didn't exactly
fall over themselves to sign up to his vision of a
brave new world of porcelain tile, although he
did attract a surprising number of supporters.

Gillette also wrote and sponsored various
publications advocating an end to competition. In
1910, for example, in a book, entitled *World
Corporation*, he announced that he had set up a

body with the aim of centralizing the world's
economy, and offered Theodore Roosevelt a
million dollars to become its president. Roosevelt
turned him down.

Gillette was able to make such a generous
offer because by this time he had amassed a large
personal fortune. In 1891 he went to work as a
salesman for the Baltimore Seal Company, whose
president, William Painter, made an enormous
amount of money through his invention of the
crimped bottle cap. Painter is said to have advised
Gillette that the way to riches was to spend time
thinking of another such inexpensive, disposable
product; and in 1895, the entrepreneur hit on the
idea that was to make his fortune and turn his
name into a household word — the disposable
razor blade.

ABOVE **The Gillette
Ranch at Calabasas
in southern California
(1929), designed in a
loose Spanish Colonial
style by Wallace Neff.
The ranch is a perfect
setting for the leisurely
pursuit of pleasure.
Sadly, Gillette had little
time to enjoy it, losing
his fortune in the 1929
Wall Street Crash and
dying three years later.**

After overcoming various technical problems, and surviving a slow start (in 1903 the Gillette Safety Razor Company sold an underwhelming fifty-one razors and 168 blades), the idea took off, and by 1913 Gillette was able to leave the enterprise in the hands of others and retire to southern California, a wealthy man. He spent much of his time dabbling in real estate, travelling abroad, and, notwithstanding the fact that capitalism had been so good to him, pursuing his goal of a centrally controlled, socially planned global economy.

In the late 1920s Gillette commissioned a big ranch house on his estate at Calabasas in southern California. His architect was Wallace Neff (1895–1982), a Los Angeles-based designer whose clients included Hollywood stars such as Charlie Chaplin, Douglas Fairbanks, King Vidor, and Harpo Marx. At the time, Neff tended to work in a loose Spanish Colonial style, and this was what he provided for King C. Gillette.

The ranch is about as far removed from the towering domes of Metropolis as it is possible to imagine. Organized around a beautiful formal patio, it is low and rambling, its shady arcades and cool interiors nestle into the hillside, while at the same time provide an exhilarating sense of space, with spectacular views over the hills near Malibu. Like so many Spanish Colonial houses, the Gillette Ranch is an invention, a romantic reinterpretation of the Mission myth. "One can bask in the sun," wrote a reviewer for *Country Life in America* in 1930, "…with no thought of the morrow, and enjoy to the full the beautiful view of the surrounding mountains." Just how its owner reconciled this sybaritic lifestyle – or indeed, his brilliant exploitation of the very economic system that he campaigned for most of his life to abolish – with his revolutionary ideas on social and political planning is rather hard to understand.

The ranch was completed in 1929. Ironically, in the very same year, King C. Gillette's mistrust of capitalism was finally confirmed when, like many others, he lost most of his fortune in the Wall Street Crash.

RIGHT **By the 1920s the Californian Arts and Crafts movement's drive to produce a distinctive regional architecture had evolved into the patios and hedonism of the Spanish Colonial revival. "One can bask in the sun… with no thought of the morrow," said** Country Life in America **of the Gillette Ranch.**

THE WILLIAMS HOUSE

Julia Morgan for Selden Williams, 1928

The Williams House in Berkeley, California, is a good example of what became of the American Arts and Crafts movement's early preoccupation with regionality. By the 1920s, the drive to replace academic convention with architectures rooted in the traditions of particular localities had itself been replaced by a cheerful and pragmatic eclecticism. The shuttered windows, pantiled roof, and creamy-white walls of the Williams House conjure up the image of a southern European villa – Californian Mission Revival meets Italianate sophistication. The result is a little conservative, a little too controlled beside

the more flamboyant romanticism of Grayoaks or the Gamble House (see pages 74 and 82). And the ideology that underpinned regionalism has gone. But the homage to California's Spanish past is still strong, and the commitment to extraordinarily high standards of craftsmanship remains.

Julia Morgan (1872–1957), who designed the Williams House, hated being referred to as a woman architect, demanding that her work be judged on its own merits. "My buildings speak for me," she said. And indeed they do. In a brilliant career that lasted nearly half a century, she designed some 800 buildings, from exquisite Craftsman

ABOVE **The street front of the Williams House on the corner of Claremont Avenue in Berkeley, California, designed by Julia Morgan for Selden and Elizabeth Glide Williams. Like a southern European villa, the exterior of the house is formal and restrained, at once suggesting privacy and promising splendour.**

ABOVE Julia Morgan is best known today as the architect of Hearst Castle, the monumental palace she designed at San Simeon for the newspaper magnate William Randolph Hearst. But Morgan designed some 800 buildings in the course of a career that lasted for half a century, ranging from Craftsman bungalows to more urbane essays in the Mediterranean and Spanish Colonial styles.

bungalows, women's clubs, and YWCAs, to what is arguably her greatest achievement – the glorious cloud-capped Xanadu of William Randolph Hearst's castle at San Simeon, to which she devoted much of her life from 1919 to 1942.

But in the context of the time, it would be disingenuous to pretend that Morgan's sex was irrelevant. In Britain, for example, the role of women in the Arts and Crafts movement was confused and contradictory. On the one hand, William Morris's involvement in revolutionary socialism brought him and many of the designers influenced by him into contact with those women active in radical politics during the 1880s and 1890s. And women are given an equality of sorts in his later Utopian writings: in *News from Nowhere* (1891) he envisions a future when "the women do what they like best, and the men are neither jealous of it or injured by it." In practice, however, women were objects to be petted, painted, and placed on pedestals, as so many stained-glass angels in a Burne-Jones window. Women designers were excluded from the more significant groupings, such as the Art-Workers' Guild, and effectively marginalized in artistic ghettoes including the Ladies' Ecclesiastical Embroidery Society. Morris himself believed that women's suffrage had to take second place to the fight for socialism. "Child-bearing makes women inferior to men," he wrote, "since a certain time of their lives they must be dependent on them. Of course we must claim absolute equality of condition between men and women... but it would be poor economy setting women to do men's work...."

In the slightly more egalitarian climate of turn-of-the-century America, there were a handful of women architects in practice, but even so, Julia Morgan's career was remarkable. Born in San Francisco, she took an engineering degree at the University of California at Berkeley in 1894 and then went on to work in the office of Bernard Maybeck, who had been her geometry professor at Berkeley. With his encouragement, she enrolled at the Ecole des Beaux-Arts in Paris, the first woman

to study architecture there – not because women had previously been prohibited, apparently, but because no woman had ever dared to enrol before. In 1902 Morgan returned to the west coast, where her early private clients were mostly female, and her work for public bodies often involved designing buildings and facilities for women, such as a campanile, library, and gymnasium for the all-women Mills College in Oakland (1903–9). But from 1910 she established herself as one of the Bay Area's leading architects, and men as well as women lined up to offer her commissions.

Morgan's early domestic buildings were clearly influenced by Maybeck, and she continued to make use of the Craftsman style when it suited her. But she was never as devoted to the design vocabulary of the Arts and Crafts movement as her mentor. To Maybeck and contemporaries like Webb, Lethaby,

RIGHT The frescoes in the garden cloister were painted by Maxine Albro, later to become famous for her murals in San Francisco public buildings. While she refused to be categorized as a "woman architect," Julia Morgan employed women artists in her work more often than most of her male colleagues.

ABOVE **Coupled columns and cusped tracery in the conservatory of the Williams House continue its Mediterranean theme, offering sanctuary from the bright Californian sunshine and recalling the loggias and balconies of Italy in the early Renaissance.**

LEFT **The elaborate traceried window in the landing above the living hall of the Williams House shows Moorish, Venetian Gothic, and perhaps Ruskinian influences. The della Robbia roundel above it was brought by Morgan from Florence.**

Stickley, and the Greene brothers, Arts and Crafts was just not *a* style — it was *the* style — the inevitable expression of a perfect way of living. Morgan's academic training left her with an approach to architecture that was at once more eclectic and more pragmatic: she was equally happy to produce rustic cottages and Palladian villas, Tyrolean lodges, and Queen Anne mansions. She gave her clients what they wanted, and if one has a criticism of her *oeuvre*, it is that too many of her buildings seem to come from the head, not the heart.

But the underlying Arts and Crafts ethos remains strong, particularly in Morgan's domestic work, and the house she designed for Selden and Elizabeth Glide Williams on Claremont Avenue in Berkeley is a case in point. The classical, reserved, cool white concrete façade has an entrance placed centrally between tiers of symmetrical windows. But the impression of severity is relieved by the elaborately carved front door, which is surrounded by faintly Art Nouveau frescoes and crowned with an ironwork balcony. This does more than merely beckon one in; it declares that the Williams House takes pride in detail.

The door opens into a living hall, that space which occupies such a fundamental role in the English Arts and Crafts movement. But there is nothing English or even especially American about it, nor indeed about any of the spaces in the house. Instead, there are marble floors, vast windows pierced with screens of Venetian Gothic tracery (a touch Ruskin would surely have approved of), Moorish cusped arches in cast stone, and a cloistered garden adorned with almost Botticellian frescoes. The interiors offer sanctuary from the sun; they break out into the gardens via balconies, expanses of traceried window, and a Gothic conservatory.

The problem with the Williams House is that it relies too much on an academic knowledge of Spanish and Italian architecture. Like Hollyhocks (see page 88), it represents a departure from the Arts and Crafts mainstream. But whereas Wright sought to create something new by extending the notion of organic architecture, Julia Morgan took refuge in existing forms. Her work here is beautiful, and Berkeley would certainly be poorer without it; but one wishes sometimes for a little less book-learning, a little more fire in the soul.

COUNTRY LIFE

The dream of the rural idyll

"Those who dwell amidst the vulgar and impossible artistry of modern villadom may visit now and then some ancient village, and in the cottages and farmhouses there be conscious of a beauty which makes their own homes appear a trivial and frivolous affair."

When the architect M. H. Baillie Scott wrote these words, on the opening page of his 1906 book *Houses and Gardens*, he was doing no more than making a value judgement shared by many of his contemporaries, one that lay right at the heart of the English Arts and Crafts movement. The countryside was good; its homes had a solidity, a stability, a sense of continuity that positively exuded moral worth. The towns and cities, on the other hand, with their expanding middle-class suburbs, were bad. They had no soul, no vigour, no style, and no substance. William Morris himself had eloquently summed up the appeal of an old house in the country in an article on Kelmscott Manor, which he wrote in 1895:

> So much has the old house grown up out of the soil and the lives of those that lived on it; needing no grand office architect, with no great longing for anything else than correctness, and to be like Julius Caesar; but some thin thread of tradition, a half-anxious sense of the delight of the meadow and acre and wood and river; a certain amount (not too much, let us hope) of common sense, a liking for making materials serve one's turn, and perhaps at bottom some little grain of sentiment.

And he went on to raise the following question: "Might we not manage to find some sympathy for all that from henceforward, or must we but shrink before the Philistine?"

The dichotomy between town and country, between Philistinism and warm, sympathetic humanity, was fundamental to Arts and Crafts ideology, and inspired most of its greatest houses. But this dichotomy dates back only to the end of

ABOVE "Cottage" furniture such as this ladderback chair, designed and made by Ernest Gimson c.1895, allowed consumers to bring a little bit of rural England into their suburban parlours.

RIGHT Sidney Barnsley (left), his fiancée Lucy Morley, Ernest Gimson (seated), and Ernest Barnsley with his wife and two daughters, photographed outside Gimson's Cotswold cottage c.1895. Like many of their contemporaries, Gimson and the Barnsleys believed that living in the country brought them closer to the heart of the craft tradition.

the eighteenth century. Before that a cottage was, in Samuel Johnson's famous definition, no more than "a mean habitation," and the countryside was either somewhere populated by unsophisticated, poor people or, at best, a place where polite society kicked its heels during the winter months, keeping half an eye on the running of its estates while it waited for spring and the chance to get back to the bright lights of London. The Romantic movement represented a fundamental shift in attitudes towards rural life (although to be fair, this view wasn't shared by everybody: the late Victorian aesthete William Hazlitt firmly believed that "There is nothing good to be had in the country, or, if there is, they will not let you have it;" and would have died before giving up his town house and access to theatres and galleries). When Keats wrote that "To one who has been long in city pent,/'Tis very sweet to look into the fair/And open face of heaven," and Wordsworth declared himself to be "A lover of the meadows and the woods,/And mountains," they were giving voice to a new sensibility which valued Nature as a positive spiritual force, and saw the countryside as a pure and innocent world, still uncorrupted by the sins of the city.

One can't deny that this eulogizing of the countryside was abject nonsense, a form of wilful blindness that turned rural poverty and deprivation into an art object for middle-class literati. The other side of the picture was put forcibly by poets like Tom Taylor, whose "Old Cottages" (1863) contrasted the picturesque golden thatch and whitewashed walls of the idealized cottage homes beloved by Romantic poets and artists with the squalid reality: "The foul miasma of their crowded rooms,/Unaired, unlit, with green damps moulded o'er,/The fever that each autumn deals its dooms/From the rank ditch that stagnates by the door..." But the architects and designers of the Arts and Crafts movement were committed participants in a Wordsworthian Romantic sensibility; and their love affair with the countryside was heightened both by an anti-urbanism born out of the sheer ugliness of the ever-expanding industrial towns, and by a feeling that rural England was fast disappearing beneath Baillie Scott's "vulgar and impossible artistry of modern villadom." Their rose-tinted idealization of country life may seem impossible to us, but at the same time, the country houses and cottages that were built as products of that sensibility are among the most beautiful architecture in Britain, and they represent the Arts and Crafts movement at its peak.

Over the Rainbow

Country Life *magazine and the British country house*

The mythologizing of the English countryside wasn't confined to the Arts and Crafts movement. By the turn of the century, William Morris's dream of a paradise that honest, decent folk had lost through the serpent-like blandishments of industrialization was common currency among the urban middle classes, who spent their weekends and summer holidays on a quest for "the real England." (Their enthusiasm was not shared by rural labourers, who forsook their squalid country cottages for the town in huge numbers.)

One day in about 1895, so the story goes, two men were playing a round of golf at Walton Heath in Surrey. One was George Riddell, a well-to-do solicitor with interests in publishing; his companion was Edward Hudson, a successful printer. As they played, the pair hit on an idea for a new, high-quality journal that would make effective use of half-tone block printing, an illustrated weekly appealing to the manufacturers and city business-men who longed – or whose wives longed – for their own home in the country. The magazine would carry articles on old country houses and

ABOVE **William Morris's bedroom at Kelmscott Manor, photographed for a *Country Life* issue on the house in 1921. Largely due to the influence of Lawrence Weaver, who was its architectural editor for most of the 1910s, the magazine became a forum for the promotion of modern Arts and Crafts architecture.**

gardens, antiques, natural history, traditional country pursuits (most of which seemed to involve killing something), and sporting occasions, such as the horse-racing at Ascot and the rowing regatta at Henley, frequented by high society.

And so *Country Life* was born. Aptly described by a modern contributor, Sir Roy Strong, as "the manual of gentrification for the late Victorian and Edwardian middle classes," its first issue appeared in January 1897, and within less than a decade it had become required reading for everyone who was – or aspired to be – part of the landed elite.

It was Edward Hudson who guided the magazine through its early years. A self-made man with little formal education, he emerges from contemporary accounts as rather sad: a socially insecure outsider with a reverence for landed society and a belief that it represented the best of England. His favourite architect was Edwin Lutyens. The two were introduced in 1899 by Gertrude Jekyll – later a regular columnist for the magazine – and in the same year Hudson commissioned Lutyens to design the Deanery Garden at Sonning in Berkshire. This romantic masterpiece in brick and timber evoked the past so perfectly that it was later advertised for sale – in *Country Life* – as "a very beautiful Elizabethan house." Hudson gave Lutyens three further commissions: the remodelling of Lindisfarne Castle (1902), the Wrenaissance *Country Life* Building in Tavistock Street, London (1904), and Plumpton Place in Sussex (1928).

Country Life's relationship with Arts and Crafts designers was ambivalent. The country house was its *beau ideal*, and the older the better: the magazine felt that from around 1840, the country house had been "allowed to stray on to very unsatisfactory lines." H. Avray Tipping, one of the most influential contributors in the early 1900s, tended to concentrate on historic buildings, although Lawrence Weaver, appointed architectural editor in 1910, promoted the work of Lethaby, Webb, and other Arts and Crafts stalwarts (see page 60).

The real importance of *Country Life* for the Arts and Crafts movement lay in the part it played in creating a particular vision of England. Ironically, considering the fact that it gloried in inherited privilege, it did as much as Morris, a socialist, to create for urban dwellers an image of a rural utopia that was almost close enough to touch, but always just out of reach.

MUNSTEAD WOOD

Edwin Lutyens for Gertrude Jekyll, 1896–7

Gertrude Jekyll knew exactly what she wanted from Munstead Wood: "My house is to be built for me to live in and love; it is not to be built as an exposition of architectonic inutility." There were to be no frills, no fancy ornament, no "specious or fashionable devices of spurious antiquity"; she wanted something "designed and built in the thorough and honest spirit of the good work of old days."

She was lucky, then – or shrewd – in her choice of architect. Like her, Edwin Lutyens (1869–1944) had a deep, abiding love for the cottages and farmhouses of Surrey and Sussex that were the inspiration behind Munstead Wood: picturesque, lopsided outcrops of brick and stone and tile that

seemed to have grown out of the soil. Just as importantly, Lutyens was young and inexperienced, with only one major commission under his belt. Jekyll could bully him. On one occasion, she simply shouted him down, recalling years later how "the architect's crushed and somewhat frightened demeanour [showed] that long words certainly have their use, if only as engines of warfare."

In general, though, the relationship between Lutyens and Jekyll was warm and affectionate. They first met in the spring of 1889 at the Surrey home of a mutual friend, the rhododendron grower Harry Mangle. Lutyens was tall, trusting, and twenty, and had set up his own practice only a month or so earlier. Jekyll was short, stern, and

ABOVE **The south front of Munstead Wood. Gertrude Jekyll's ground-floor living hall is in the centre, with her book room to the left and dining room to the right. There is nothing folksy or quaint here, just a respect for the past – a reflection of Jekyll's desire for a home whose new walls should quickly take on "the soul of a more ancient dwelling place."**

forty-five — "a bunch of cloaked propriety topped by a black felt hat," Lutyens called her — and already beginning to establish a reputation for herself as a garden designer, an occupation she had taken up when failing eyesight forced her to give up a career as a painter, silverworker, and embroideress. She was living with her mother at Munstead House, south of Godalming, and was laying out her famous fifteen-acre garden on a plot she had bought some years earlier, just across the road from the family home.

The couple got on immediately, largely as a result of their shared interest in the vernacular architecture of Surrey and Sussex. During the early 1890s they spent many weekends together, bowling along country lanes in Jekyll's pony cart, hunting for old farms and tumbledown cottages. Moreover, the friendship, which lasted until Gertrude's death in 1932, quickly turned into a professional collaboration. Within months of their first meeting, "Aunt Bumps," as the young architect christened her, was advising on the layout of the gardens at Lutyens's first big commission,

Crooksbury near Farnham (1890), Surrey, a thoroughly Old English mixture of tile hanging, half-timbering, and Tudor chimneys, designed for Harry Mangle's sister and her husband. Other cooperative ventures soon followed.

In 1894 Lutyens drew up plans for a small cottage in the midst of Jekyll's gardens at Munstead. The Hut was stark and simple, with whitewashed walls, brick floors, and the inevitable inglenook — the perfect setting in which to act out the fantasy folk rituals so beloved of the early Arts and Crafts movement. On winter evenings, Jekyll and her friends liked to sit by the fire, drinking hot elderberry wine and singing folk songs.

The Hut was never meant to be a permanent home, so late in 1895 Lutyens began work on the designs for a larger building. The new house was still small by the standards of the day, consisting of a living hall, dining room, book room,

BELOW **Munstead Wood garden. "It is important,"** wrote Jekyll, "in such a border of rather large size... to keep the flowers in rather large masses of colour."

workshop, and domestic offices on the ground floor, with four main bedrooms above. But it was much more sophisticated than the Hut, showing a fidelity to materials, craftsmanship, and the local vernacular that placed it firmly within the Arts and Crafts tradition; at the same time, it also marked a new maturity and sensitivity in Lutyens's work. The walls are mainly of local Bargate stone, topped with handmade red tiles and crowned with huge chimneystacks, a picturesque feature that again shows his early debt to the Old English style of Richard Norman Shaw. So, too, does the wide half-timbered gallery, which breaks out to the north, giving access to the first-floor rooms and lit by a narrow horizontal band of leaded casements.

The windows are generally quite small throughout the house, making the interiors dark and almost gloomy. This was a "fault" in the design for which Lutyens was roundly criticized by contemporaries, who didn't understand that sunlight was deliberately excluded because, with her failing eyesight, Jekyll found it painful. In fact, the low lighting levels give Munstead a feeling of almost womblike comfort and security, an impression that is enhanced by the low oak-beamed ceilings and the simple, unpretentious detailing: the massive canopied chimneypiece in the living hall, the broad shallow steps of the oak staircase, the massive exposed timbers of the gallery.

Within a few years of designing Munstead Wood, Lutyens had begun to move away from his free Arts and Crafts style towards the formal symmetries of the Edwardian Wrenaissance, a journey that would culminate in the monumental classicism of New Delhi. Never one to share the political and ideological outlook of Morris and Webb, he was perhaps more at home when working in a style influenced by aristocratic affluence and imperial grandeur. But as homes go, Munstead Wood's quiet domesticity seems infinitely preferable to the pretension of a millionaire's mansion, or the stiff splendours of a vice-regal's palace.

RIGHT **The living hall as it was in 1907, with Lutyens's massive and faintly Gothic canopied chimneypiece and, to the right, Jekyll's aspidistra – a surprisingly bourgeois touch, perhaps, for such a revolutionary gardener. The unpretentious staircase, which leads up to an oak-beamed first-floor gallery, was one of Gertrude's favourite features: "It felt firm and solid," she said, "the steps low and broad."**

THE ARTS AND CRAFTS GARDEN

Imagine yourself for a moment back in the 1860s, taking a leisurely stroll through the gardens of a small country house. What would you find? Dark laurel and rhododendron crowding in on straight gravel walks; flowerbeds laid out in fantastically elaborate patterns like paper doilies; relentless symmetry and fussy formality.

What you wouldn't find is the slightest concession to nature. High Victorian designers were united in their insistence that there was no room for natural forms in the garden. They agreed with Edward Kemp, who in his influential *How to Lay Out a Garden* (1850) declared that flowerbeds "ought never to be scattered, as it were, broadcast over a lawn, without any connection...they should always fall into some regular figure." The equally influential J. C. Loudon, whose *Suburban Gardener and Villa Companion* (1836) became a bible for the gardening middle classes, was just as dogmatic in championing the artificial, stating that "Forms

perfectly regular, and divisions completely uniform, immediately excite the belief of design and, with this belief, all the admiration which follows the employment of skill."

But by the 1880s such ideas had been challenged – and rejected – everywhere except for a few conservative outposts in the Pooterish suburbs. The assault had come on several fronts. Led by William Robinson (1838–1935), author of *The English Flower Garden* (1883) and owner-editor of *Gardening* magazine, gardeners themselves rebelled against the artificial nature of the High Victorian style. "Natural grouping is the true and artistic way," wrote Robinson, who advocated using wild flowers and called on gardeners to break free of "barren geometry." Although his own schemes were considerably less radical than his writings implied, those writings had a tremendous impact. In the visual arts, the paintings of Helen Allingham, Myles Birket Foster, and other members of the Witley School presented an idealized rural imagery that popularized the cottage gardens of Kent and Surrey, the horticultural equivalents of the Arts and Crafts movement's picturesque vernacular architecture. Allingham's most characteristic work is to be seen in the elegiac book *Cottage Homes of England* (1909), accompanying Stewart Dick's lyrical descriptions of the cottage garden: "Tall hollyhocks reaching almost to the thatched eaves, sweet-smelling wallflowers spreading their fragrance far out into the dusty road..."

The name most often associated with the turn-of-the-century revolution in garden design is that of Gertrude Jekyll (1843–1932). Between 1880, when she produced one of her first planting schemes, for her mother's Munstead House in Surrey, and her death, she received some 400 gardening commissions and wrote nearly 2,000 articles and fifteen full-length books. In the process, she did more than most to raise gardening to an art form, bringing together art and horticulture in the same way that Morris and his colleagues sought a union between arts and crafts.

LEFT **The matronly figure of Gertrude Jekyll walking in the Spring Garden at Munstead Wood, Surrey, in the early 1920s. The doyenne of British garden designers, Jekyll championed the idea of the artist-gardener as the horticultural counterpart of the artist/craftsman.**

ABOVE **The Well Court at Snowshill Manor, Gloucestershire.** Snowshill's gardens were laid out in 1920–3 as a series of enclosed interconnecting spaces by their owner, Charles Wade, to a design by M. H. Baillie Scott. "A garden is an extension of the house," Wade wrote, "a series of outdoor rooms... never show all there is at once."

One of the ways in which Jekyll achieved this was by bringing an artist's eye for colour to her planting plans. As she explained in *Colour Schemes for the Flower Garden* (1908), "When the eye is trained to perceive pictorial effect, it is frequently struck by something — some combination of grouping, lighting, and colour — that is seen to have that complete aspect of unity and beauty that to the artist's eye forms a picture. Such are the impressions that the artist/gardener endeavours to produce in every portion of the garden." In a typical Jekyll garden, long borders filled with large masses and drift-planting at a slight angle to a path give the appearance of natural groupings. Plants are banked with the tallest at the back; "receding" colours such as blues and violets also tend to be placed furthest away from the observer, with warm "advancing" colours — reds and oranges — at the front. The single-colour borders of blue, grey, white, or gold are often accentuated by a dash of a complementary colour, a group of white lilies or something "of palest lemon-yellow" in a blue garden, for instance. "Any experienced colourist knows that the blues will be more telling — more purely blue — by the juxtaposition of the rightly placed complementary colour", as Jekyll noted.

LEFT Structural planting at Tintinhull House garden, Somerset, laid out at the turn of the century and replanted in the 1930s. Many Edwardian architects and their clients favoured what Lutyens described as "the simple dignity and sweetness and quiet beauty of the old formal garden."

The history of Jekyll's partnership with Edwin Lutyens, in which he produced the structural plan for a garden and she was responsible for the planting, is discussed earlier in this chapter. In the early 1900s Lutyens moved away from the romantic Arts and Crafts style he had so lovingly produced at Munstead Wood (see page 110) towards a much stricter Wrenaissance classicism, exemplified by grandiose country houses like Nashdom in Buckinghamshire (1905–9) and William-and-Mary lookalikes such as the Salutation in Kent (1911). As he did so, his working relationship with Jekyll became increasingly problematic. His enthusiasm for what Jekyll herself described as "the simple dignity and sweetness and quiet beauty of the old formal garden" was ill suited to her own much more impressionistic and naturalistic approach, and this dichotomy came to mirror the tensions that existed between many Arts and Crafts architects and artist-gardeners of the period. The architects, even those whose houses recalled the rambling, asymmetrical buildings of the past, tended to favour the type of garden that relied on a strong structural framework; planting was secondary to the built skeleton. The artist/gardener, on the other hand, used plants to create form and structure. (The working gardener, incidentally, didn't get a look in – the movement's reverence for traditional craftsmen didn't extend to him.)

Arguing in 1896 for a synthesis of formal and free gardening styles, Jekyll noted that "the formal army are architects to a man." Even the most avid Arts and Crafts architects surrounded their essentially Romantic buildings with surprisingly formal gardens, which drew on late seventeenth- and early eighteenth-century high-status landscapes, and seem at odds with the organic qualities of the Arts and Crafts house. At Wightwick Manor

LEFT Planting takes second place to stone ornament in the Italianate gardens at Iford Manor in Wiltshire, created by the country house architect Harold Peto in the early years of the twentieth century.

BELOW **The pergola at Gertrude Jekyll's Munstead Wood, looking towards the main flower garden. Jekyll was not afraid to use straight lines and architectural forms where appropriate, aiming for a synthesis of formal and free gardening styles.**

(see page 26), Thomas Mawson, who was called in after Flora Mander saw a copy of his *Art and Craft of Garden Making* (1898), produced a scheme that made use of balustraded terraces, clipped yew hedges, and strong axial vistas; he held that "to give a proper connection between the house and garden a formal arrangement near the house is essential." At Melsetter House (see page 34), W. R. Lethaby also introduced clipped yew and straight green walks, and a parterre filled with beds laid out in amazingly convoluted patterns. And E. S. Prior, who argued that "since man walks straight from point to point – unless intoxicated – a bend or a curve certainly requires excuse for its eccentricity," gave Home Place (see page 130) rigidly geometrical walks and alleys, terraces, and sunken gardens.

Gardens are transient things. One of the best Arts and Crafts examples to survive reasonably intact is at Snowshill Manor in Gloucestershire, a Cotswold manor house in an attractive mix of Tudor and early Georgian styles, which was bought in 1919 by the architect and collector Charles Paged Wade (1883–1956). Wade deliberately eschewed any horticultural advice and made no bones about his priorities. "A garden is an extension of the house," he wrote, "...a delightful garden can be made in which flowers play a very small part, by using effects of light and shade, vistas, steps to changing levels, terraces, walls, fountains, running water, an old well head or a statue in the right place." With help from the architect M. H. Baillie Scott, he made just this type of garden at Snowshill, clearing an old farmyard on the hillside behind the house to create a series of walled outdoor "rooms" on different levels. It all works perfectly – proof that at its best the Arts and Crafts garden has a beauty and tranquillity that transcend its apparent contradictions.

BROADLEYS

C. F. A. Voysey for Arthur Briggs, 1898–1900

Charles Francis Annesley Voysey (1857–1941) doesn't really fit the Morris/Webb/Lethaby mould of Arts and Crafts architects. He was certainly earnest enough, but his earnestness took him along a somewhat different path. In politics, for instance, he was a libertarian right-winger who hated trade unions because they "interfere unduly with the workman's sentiments, much to his degradation," and held that if one would only appeal privately to the bricklayer's moral sense, "he will respond at once, and see the advantage to himself and others of cultivating individual enterprise and self-respect." Voysey's hostility extended towards all forms of collectivism, which he saw as stifling individual creativity; and although he joined the Art Workers' Guild shortly after its foundation in 1884, he generally went his own way, steering clear of the groupings and artistic communities that proliferated at the end of the century. He also held strong religious convictions, although these too

seem to have been out of the cultural mainstream, since they were handed down from his clergyman father, who founded his own church after being cast out of the Church of England for refusing to accept the doctrine of eternal damnation.

Voysey's architectural principles were as high-minded as his political and religious beliefs, although rather less controversial. The qualities one should look for in a home, he said, were "repose, cheerfulness, simplicity, breadth, warmth, quietness in storm, economy of up-keep, evidence of protection, harmony with surroundings, absence of dark passages or places, evenness of temperature." This idea of quiet domesticity governs his houses. They tend to be plain because, in order to achieve repose, it was necessary to avoid "angularity and complexity in colour, form or texture." They hug the ground, with dominant horizontal lines: "When the sun sets, horizontalism prevails, when we are weary we recline." The doors are often wide in proportion to their height, because this suggested welcome. "The cottage is [Voysey's] ideal," wrote Hermann Muthesius in 1904, "even when he is building houses of a size and luxuriousness more appropriate to a palace."

Broadleys, which stands on a spectacular site overlooking Lake Windermere in the English Lake District, is neither a cottage nor a palace, but it does embody the domestic virtues that Voysey held so dear. It was designed in 1898 for Arthur Currer Briggs, whose family had made their money from coal mining in Yorkshire. Briggs lived in Leeds and wanted a retreat for weekends and summer holidays in the fashionable Lake District, just over a hundred miles away but easily accessible by train. Voysey was in his early forties, with seventeen years' experience in independent

ABOVE This carved grotesque head, which is one of two corbels supporting the gallery overlooking the living hall at Broadleys, is reputed to be a portrait of Voysey's client, Arthur Currer Briggs.

LEFT Portrait of Charles Francis Annesley Voysey by Harold Speed, 1896. Voysey was a determined individualist who developed a distinctive architectural style early on in his career, to which he gradually became a prisoner.

ABOVE **Presentation drawing of Broadleys by Howard Gaye, 1898, showing the three bow windows of the dining room, hall, and drawing room, which look west out across Lake Windermere. The entrance court and service wing lie to the east; the open verandah at the south end of the main block has since been filled in.**

practice and nearly twenty residential commissions to his credit, most of them either small cottages or substantial houses – stylish but not too grand – for just the type of *haut bourgeois* client epitomized by Briggs.

Briggs knew exactly the sort of house Voysey would give him. To quote Muthesius again: "Voysey almost invariably uses rough plaster on his walls and English slate for his roofs. He often places broad, tapering buttresses at the corners, his roofs project a long way beyond the walls and usually rest on slender wrought-iron brackets. His fenestration consists of strips of small, narrow windows..." All of these features are present in Broadleys. In fact, if Voysey has a fault, it is that they are present rather too often in his buildings. Once he had established his distinctive style, he became its prisoner. Clients came to him because they wanted a Voysey house; they knew what a Voysey house should look like – and, no matter

RIGHT **Little lead hearts set into the balusters of the staircase. Voysey often employed this whimsical and faintly emetic motif in the decoration of his buildings: next to the garden door of his own house, the Orchard (1899), he even trained the ivy which climbed the wall into the shape of a heart.**

where they lived, a Voysey house was what they got, complete with roughcast walls, tapering buttresses, and sweeping roofs. Even if in theory, he shared his contemporaries' respect for the vernacular, he was allowed to make few concessions to local building traditions, a fact which he seems to have found quite frustrating. Aymer Valance, writing in *The Studio* in 1904, reported Voysey's regret that his clients always insisted on having "what he or she deems a thoroughly characteristic house instead of one more properly native to the soil."

A thoroughly characteristic house is what Voysey designed for Briggs at Broadleys. Not that he was a mail-order architect: between May 1898, when he first made the long journey up from his London office to look over the site, and December 1900, when Broadleys was finished, he paid twenty-three visits to the Lake District, as well as making two further trips up to Leeds to consult with Briggs. At the time he was also designing Moorcrag, another holiday home on Windermere for another industrialist, J. W. Buckley, and he often combined his site visits. (He also charged full travelling expenses to both clients – a petty dishonesty that, given Voysey's propensity for taking the moral high ground, is somehow terribly disappointing.) By October 1898, Voysey and Briggs had agreed on the design, and Howard Gaye was paid two guineas to produce a presentation painting.

Above a rather forbidding stone-walled terrace brightened with sunflowers, Gaye's perspective focuses on the west façade, which understandably looks onto Lake Windermere to make the best of the views. For a moment, the three bow windows that break through the roofline conjure up memories of Regency terraces in Bognor or Brighton. But Voysey, who went further than most Arts and Crafts architects to avoid any hint of historicism, was careful to dispel this impression with deliberate touches of asymmetry, adding broad white chimneystacks at different heights, and a south-facing verandah at one end.

The ground floor of this main, west-facing block is almost entirely taken up with three reception rooms, each with their own curving bow and hence with their own view over the lake: the dining room, the drawing room, and, between them, a large living hall complete with billiard table and inglenook fireplace. The main staircase rises behind and to one side of the hall, tucked in at the back of the drawing room. A low service wing stretches away to the east on one side, giving the house an L-shaped ground plan in which the entrance façade, a rather magnificent assembly of receding and advancing gables and bays, fills the short arm of the L.

The drawing room and dining room are both quite low, with beamed ceilings and fire surrounds of glazed tiles; both rooms have a self-consciously cottagey feel to them – especially the dining room, which has oak panelling and plenty of shelves for

displaying plates, china, and ornaments. The living hall in the centre of the house rises up the full height of the building; it has a glazed corridor at first-floor level which, like the bow windows, recalls the past – suggesting the minstrel gallery of a medieval great hall – while at the same time rejecting it: the glazing is too modern, the whole composition too horizontal to masquerade as a quaint Old English feature.

Broadleys is also notable for the light touches that became something of a trademark in Voysey houses, as if the architect felt the need to provide relief from the austerity of his interiors. The two corbels that support the gallery, for example, are decorated with grotesque carved heads, which are probably portraits of Arthur Briggs. Also, the balusters of the staircase are inlaid with little lead hearts, a motif that occurs in many of Voysey's buildings. The effect of both these decorative devices is either pleasantly playful or mildly tiresome, depending on your mood.

ABOVE **The double-height living hall, which occupies the centre of the main block. The bow window with its curving seat is set back behind what almost amounts to a proscenium arch, which vies for attention with a wide inglenook fireplace.**

RIGHT **The verticality of the staircase, behind and to one side of the hall, is emphasized by newel-posts that extend until they reach the ceiling. The underlying atmosphere, said Muthesius, "is one of delicate, almost timid, modesty."**

STONEYWELL COTTAGE

Ernest Gimson for Sydney Gimson, 1898–9

In 1910, in his book *Small Country Houses of Today*, Lawrence Weaver reviewed the thatched stone cottage that the craftsman/designer Ernest Gimson (1864–1919) had built for himself at Sapperton in Gloucestershire in 1902. Weaver was extremely impressed with what he saw:

> There is nowhere the obtrusion of a good feature overdone, nowhere the jar of a bad one half hidden away…There is no feature, no material, no workmanship that sets out to be ornamental, none that fails to be charming. The impression carried away is that the accommodation and the disposition

desired were carried out in materials close at hand, and fell into the shape and assumed the appearance before us out of the sheer necessity of the case. It all looks as clear and simple as that two and two make four, and that is why it is a triumph.

Nine years later, in the second volume of *Small Country Houses*, Weaver wrote up Stoneywell Cottage, a summer retreat — also thatched, also built of rough-hewn stone — created by Gimson at Ulverscroft on the edge of Charnwood Forest, about five miles north-west of his home town of Leicester. But now Weaver was less sure. The interiors were so restrained and sparse, the setting

ABOVE **Stoneywell Cottage, designed by Ernest Gimson for his brother Sydney; Detmar Blow acted as clerk of works. Stoneywell's rugged, organic quality, which makes it seem like a sleeping giant nestling among the rocks, unsettled Gimson's contemporaries. Lawrence Weaver described the house as "an unusual product of the building art."**

ABOVE A brass candle sconce designed by Ernest Gimson, c.1906. It was made in the 1930s by Norman Bucknell, carrying on a tradition established by his blacksmith father, Alfred, who was one of Gimson's favourite metalworkers.

so exposed and remote, as to be almost monastically austere. Stoneywell was, Weaver confessed, "frankly an unusual product of the building art."

Stoneywell predates the Sapperton house by three or four years. It was one of five cottages designed by Gimson at Ulverscroft between 1897 and 1908. The first pair, for James Bilson, have since been altered out of all recognition. The second pair, Stoneywell and its companion Lea Cottage, were built in 1898–9 for Gimson's brothers, Sydney and Mentor, with Detmar Blow acting as clerk of works; the fifth and smallest cottage, completed in 1908 at a cost of £600 (about $950), was for his sister Margaret.

Although Gimson's reputation rests largely on his furniture, metalwork, and plasterwork, he first trained as an architect with J. D. Sedding, whose Oxford Street office was next door to the showrooms of Morris & Co. (It was Morris who recommended Gimson to Sedding, after meeting him as a nineteen-year-old at his parents' home.)

Gimson's fellow pupil in Sedding's office was Ernest Barnsley, and it was through Ernest's brother Sidney, who worked in Richard Norman Shaw's practice alongside W. R. Lethaby, that he became part of the circle of young Arts and Crafts architects who gathered around Shaw in the 1880s. In 1890, inspired by a series of lectures at the Art-Workers' Guild, Gimson decided to devote himself to crafts rather than architecture, and the same year, in partnership with four other architects (Lethaby, Sidney Barnsley, Mervyn Macartney, and Reginald Blomfield), he set up the firm of Kenton & Co. "with the object of supplying furniture of good design and good workmanship." The venture wasn't a success — commercially at least, although between them, the five made some very beautiful furniture — and Kenton & Co. was disbanded eighteen months later. Gimson and the two Barnsley brothers soon decamped to the Cotswolds, in an attempt to get closer to the source of traditional rural crafts.

Gimson's small architectural output dates mainly from 1892 to 1910. Apart from two fairly ordinary Webb-inspired houses in Leicester and the design for the library at Bedales School in Hampshire, built posthumously under Sidney Barnsley's supervision in 1920, it consisted largely of a series of almost puritanically plain thatched cottages. There was the Charnwood Forest group, Sapperton, and Coxen, a thatch-and-cob house at Budleigh Salterton in Devon, built for Gimson's blacksmith, Basil Young, in 1910. Sapperton is perhaps the prettiest of his houses, but Stoneywell is the best, and the most thought-provoking.

The plan is deceptively simple. The front door opens into a big, traditional kitchen, with a semi-circular stair turret opposite. The sitting room is on the left, a storage area on the right, and bedrooms up above. The main rooms were originally whitewashed, with furniture and fittings supplied by Gimson and the Barnsleys: a plain country table and ladder-back chairs, an oak kitchen cupboard by Ernest Barnsley, and a wagon-back bed, also in English oak, by his brother Sidney.

LEFT A stained oak dresser by Ernest Gimson, c.1902-5. Gimson is best known today for his furniture designs, although like many Arts and Crafts designers from William Morris onwards, he originally trained as an architect.

But Gimson gave a twist — quite literally — to the orthodox cottage layout that could be found almost anywhere in England, by setting both ends of the building at roughly 45-degree angles to the centre, forming a zigzag. Moreover, the three elements of this tripartite zigzag bear little relation to the three rooms inside, so the sitting room is bent round a corner to meet the wall of the kitchen, and the kitchen bends again to meet the storage shed. Because there are so few rooms, there is no fussiness or self-conscious cleverness about this arrangement. Instead, it seems entirely natural, as if the cottage were folding itself into the surrounding countryside.

This is in part the secret of Stoneywell's success. The house seems to lie half-buried in the hillside, like some primeval creature struggling to emerge from the landscape that imprisons it. As Peter Davey says in his classic study *Arts and Crafts Architecture*, "If nature made buildings, they would surely look something like Stoneywell." The massive chimneystack in the sitting room seems to reinforce this mood, projecting out from the southern end of the house as if it were a natural outcrop of rock.

Lawrence Weaver's description of Stoneywell as "an unusual product of the building art" shows his unease at this blurring of conventional boundaries. But what he failed to understand was the extent to which Gimson was playing with the idea of the country cottage, a building type that was fast achieving almost mythic status in late-Victorian England. (Although not in Scotland, Wales, or Ireland, where it tended to be regarded less romantically as a house lived in by poor people.) It was a symbol of the simple life, a sanctuary of innocence, a safe refuge from the ills of modern civilization. With Stoneywell, Gimson took these ideas one step further, turning the symbol into stone, stripping away its chocolate-box prettiness, and in the process creating an organic, natural architecture that most other Arts and Crafts designers aspired to, but never achieved.

RIGHT **The interior of Stoneywell. Low beams and plain whitewashed walls, "cottage" furniture, and the narrow, sinuous curve of the staircase all help Stoneywell create the impression of a quiet, almost primitive escape from the hustle and bustle of the city.**

EDEN IN SUBURBIA

Urban development and Arts and Crafts ideology

One of the problems for socially concerned Arts and Crafts architects at the end of the nineteenth century was finding the right response to urban architecture. The town was bad, the countryside good – by now that was a cultural commonplace. One possible answer lay in the small rural town, which was close enough to the countryside, and therefore to the past, to absorb the sort of buildings they wanted to design. It was unspoiled by factory smoke, perhaps still dotted with Tudor, Stuart, and Georgian buildings, and the squalor in which its poorer inhabitants lived was decently hidden behind the doors of just the sort of picturesque cottages they were intent on creating.

Cities were an entirely different matter. If they were radical enough, the architects might well share Morris's dream of a future when all England was to become a garden, "with all the necessary dwellings, sheds, and workshops scattered up and down the country, all trim and neat and pretty." But they knew this wasn't going to happen overnight. If they weren't simply to ignore the city – and both Ruskin and Morris told them that to do so was morally unacceptable – they had to find an architectural idiom that brought integrity and passion back into urban and suburban housing.

For a time in the 1870s and 1880s, the Queen Anne Revival seemed to offer just such an idiom. Harking back in a vague way to the pretty red brick and white sash windows of the early eighteenth century, it provided a bright, clean, pre-industrial image that was quite different from the ponderous Gothic favoured by the previous generation, and far more attractive than the unimaginative catch-all classicism that still characterized a great deal of bourgeois housing.

RIGHT **Bath Road in Bedford Park, an idyll of white paint and red brick as depicted by the artist B. F. Berry in 1882. "Thus was a village builded,"** recorded the 1881 *Ballad of Bedford Park*, **"For all who are aesthete,/Whose precious souls it fill did/With utter joy complete."**

Queen Anne can be seen en masse at Bedford Park, just north of Chiswick in west London. It was here in 1875 that an idealistic entrepreneur, Jonathan T. Carr, converted the open fields around his father-in-law's eighteenth-century house into a spacious suburban "village" for the progressive middle classes. The original joint architects for the development were E. W. Godwin and the firm of Coe & Robinson, but the latter proved too staid for Carr, and the former perhaps too advanced: Godwin had spent the previous seven years living in sin with the actress Ellen Terry, which tended to keep respectable clients away. Although both Godwin and Coe & Robinson built a number of houses on the estate, by 1877 they had been replaced by Richard Norman Shaw, at that time an enthusiastic exponent of Queen Anne. Under his supervision, Bedford Park acquired around 500 detached and semi-detached houses, each with "A Garden and a Bath Room with Hot and Cold Water," according to an 1881 prospectus, which proclaimed the estate to be "The Healthiest Place in the World." Shaw also designed the Church of St Michael and All Angels — a rather Old English composition, but topped with a Baroque cupola — and the quaintly Chaucerian Tabard Inn, decorated with tiles by Walter Crane and William de Morgan. There were two schools (one for the children of fashionably agnostic parents and the other for those of equally fashionable High Church ritualists), together with a school of art, a cooperative store, a tennis court, and a clubhouse that admitted women as well as men. The whole enterprise was lampooned in an

LEFT **Picturesque Old English at Bournville, a low-density housing development designed as a model village by the Quaker Cadbury family. Intended primarily for workers at Cadbury's chocolate factory, cottages were also rented to outsiders in an attempt to create a more mixed community.**

article called "The Ballad of Bedford Park," which appeared in *The St James' Gazette* in 1881: "With red and blue and sagest green/were walls and dado dyed,/ Friezes of Morris there were seen and oaken wainscot wide."

Bedford Park was, as Carr proclaimed, "the most conspicuous effort yet made to break the dull dreariness of the ordinary suburban villa." It attracted a progressive set of occupants, from actors and artists, writers and architects, to Fenian revolutionaries and Russian anarchists. Yet charming though it was, there was something irredeemably unreal about Bedford Park, with all its aesthetes and anarchists and Anglo-Catholics playing tennis together or discussing dress reform in the Tabard, its pretty little Kate Greenaway children bowling their hoops down its meticulously swept streets, and — let's be honest — its air of smug superiority.

For a corrective to this aesthetes' elysium, we can turn briefly to the model communities built by philanthropic capitalists for their workers at the turn of the century. Paternalistic they may have been, but ironically they were also much more in tune with the political radicalism of the Arts and Crafts movement than a bourgeois haven like

BELOW **This house, with its four bedrooms, nurseries, and hot-air central heating, is typical of the spacious, vaguely artistic-looking homes for the professional classes that were Bedford Park's speciality. It was designed by E. J. May (1853–1941), who replaced Richard Shaw as consulting architect in about 1879.**

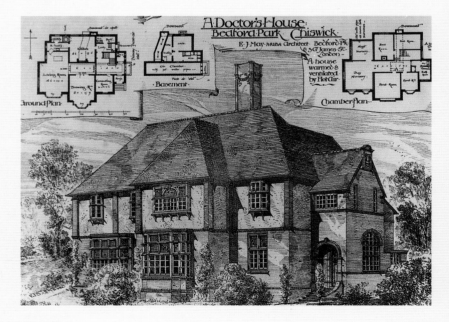

ABOVE The parlour
of a cottage in New
Earswick, the model
village laid out from
1902 onwards for
Joseph Rowntree's
workers by architects
Barry Parker and
Raymond Unwin.
In 1907, when the
photograph was taken,
the weekly rent on this
particular cottage was
six shillings and
sixpence (32.5p,
or about 10¢).

Bedford Park, much closer to Ruskin's definition of a real home as "not the number so-and-so Paradise Row, but a cottage all of our own, with its little garden, its healthy air, its clean kitchen, parlour and bedrooms." The most famous are the Bournville estate in Birmingham, begun in 1879 for the workers in Cadbury's chocolate factory; the soap manufacturer W. H. Lever's Port Sunlight in Cheshire (1888 onwards); and Joseph Rowntree's New Earswick near York (1902 onwards).

Architecturally, they are rather a mixed bag. Both Bournville and Port Sunlight owed a lot to the Old English of Shaw and William Eden Nesfield, with jettied upper storeys and timber-framed gables. New Earswick is rather more interesting. The supervising architects were Barry Parker (1867–1947) and Raymond Unwin (1863–1940), pioneers of town planning as social engineering and best known for their designs for the first garden city at Letchworth in Hertfordshire (1903). For Rowntree, who wanted houses that were "artistic in appearance, sanitary, well-built, and yet within the means of men earning about twenty-five shillings a week" (about £1.10 or 60¢), they produced a delightful variety of cottages, all with gardens, grouped around a triangular village green. Some were of brick, others had roughcast exteriors. There were dormers and gables, built-in cupboards, and colour-washed internal walls. Earswick showed that, given the political will and the financial backing, the Arts and Crafts movement could provide a decent, practical, and good-looking solution to the problem of overcrowded city tenements.

HOME PLACE

Edward Schroeder Prior for the Rev. Percy Lloyd, 1903–5

ome Place, said a nervous Lawrence
Weaver in 1909, "does not fall readily
into any defined architectural category."
Country Life's architectural editor just didn't know
what to make of the house. It wasn't Gothic, it
wasn't classical. It didn't really borrow from the
local vernacular, but nor did it show any signs of
the stripped-down modernist aesthetic currently
being developed in Europe. And the materials it
was made from – flint and concrete walls edged
with sandstone and decorated with pebbles and
haphazard geometrical patterns of thin, red tile
bricks – were not what one expected in a residence
built for an Edwardian clergyman. He eventually
decided rather coyly that it was like "a vivacious
maiden" dressed in brilliant colours: "Her very
exuberance may jar on elder nerves, but we are
nonetheless conscious of freshness and beauty."

Colourful, exuberant – even downright weird
– Home Place has delighted and confused since
1903, when its oddly splayed wings first rose up
out of a turnip field a few miles inland from the
bleak north Norfolk coast. In 1962 the historian
Nikolaus Pevsner called it "most violently idiosyncratic," admitting that it "defeats description."
More recent critics have remarked on its strangely
foreign quality, or stressed its eccentricity and the
way it stands outside the mainstream of English
architectural history. It is above all a very personal
statement of Arts and Crafts theory, and a building
that pushes that theory to its limits and beyond.

The personality behind Home Place is the
architect Edward Schroeder Prior (1852–1932).
A well-to-do barrister's son, educated at Harrow
and Cambridge, Prior excelled at athletics, gaining
awards in long jump, high jump, and hurdles, and
becoming the British amateur high jump champion
in 1872. When he came down from Cambridge in
1874 he joined the office of Richard Norman
Shaw, where he had a reputation less for his design
skills than for his public-school capers, on one
occasion wrapping up a colleague in brown paper
and leaving him out in the entrance lobby.

In 1880 Prior set up a practice for himself and, as
usual, Shaw put a commission his way as a leaving
present: Carr Manor in Leeds. For the next twenty
years Prior's connections kept him busy: a house
in Harrow for his brother; a laundry and
"Workers' Dining Hall" for his old school; repairs
to a cousin's church in Burton Bradstock, Dorset;
college buildings at Cambridge. These varied
designs show an equal facility in any one of the
styles Shaw and his office were producing in the
1870s, although it seemed that Gothic was really
where Prior's stylistic loyalties lay. His first book,
A History of Gothic Art in England (1900) was well
received. There followed three works in similar vein,
and by 1912 his scholarly reputation was enough to
secure him the Slade Chair of Art at Cambridge,
a post he held until his death. With the coming of
World War I, he all but gave up the practice of
architecture to concentrate on his academic career.

But this is only part of the story. Prior was an
ardent disciple of Morris, one of the founders of
the Art-Workers' Guild, and was also active in
other Arts and Crafts organizations. He became
interested in the idea that contemporary designers
must reject historicism and seek new idioms
dictated by the materials they worked with – and
that these idioms must be personal to the
individual. "Each artist is a school of himself," he
wrote in 1898, "with a rise, a flourish, perhaps a
decadence – and then complete extinction; he can
hand on no torch to his successor."

Prior had the chance to work out these ideas
in three buildings he designed from the mid-1890s
onwards: The Barn, Exmouth (1896), Home
Place (1903–5), and the church of St Andrew's,
Roker, near Sunderland (1906). With its spare
Gothic forms, fixtures and furniture by Gimson,

RIGHT **The south front of Home Place, Norfolk
(1903–5), designed by E. S. Prior for the Rev.
Percy Lloyd. Variously described as "impossible to
categorize," "un-English," and "violently idiosyncratic,"
Home Place is Prior's finest house, and one of the
landmarks of the English Arts and Crafts movement.**

stained glass by Henry Payne, and textiles by Morris & Co, St Andrew's is rightly regarded as his masterpiece. But Home Place is more fun.

The house sprang quite literally from the soil of Norfolk. Because of the exposed site, Prior excavated a one-acre sunken garden to a depth of some 2m (6ft) and allowed the flint, gravel, and sand he found there to govern the design. It kept the costs down, he said, with a breathtaking lack of regard for the truth. Nonetheless, this method of construction accorded with Prior's theory that what made Gothic architecture great was the fact that medieval builders had, above all, to consider "economy of materials." He also made use of direct labour, believing that contractors were an unnecessary expense and interfered with the creative relationship between architect and crafts-man. (Prior's site clerk was Randall Wells, who later achieved fame as an Arts and Crafts architect in his own right, and notoriety when he ran off with the aristocratic wife of a client.) The larger flints found on site were used for external facings, the smaller went into concrete for the walls, and the fine sand was used for mortar. Pantiles for the

roof and tile bricks for the dressings initially came from a local brickyard (although when supplies ran out Prior was forced to go further afield, to Cambridgeshire); oak for the internal joinery and the roof timbers was obtained locally; and the sandstone for quoins and window dressings came from quarries in west Norfolk.

Apart from the materials Prior used — perfectly sensible in theory, but decidedly quirky when one sees how they were transmuted into curves and angles festooned with lozenges and zigzags — Home Place's oddness also stems from its distinctive butterfly plan, in which the wings of a truncated H-shape are broken and spread apart at an angle of 120 degrees or so from the central crossbar. He had already used this idea at The Barn a few years earlier, and indeed, it enjoyed quite a vogue around the turn of the century, featured in houses by Detmar Blow and Lutyens, among others. At Home Place, the crossbar is a double-height living hall with an inglenook on its north wall. To the south, and fronting onto a terrace leading down to the sunken garden, a corridor links the hall to the dining room in one

LEFT **The main staircase, photographed (like the picture opposite) for an article that appeared in** Country Life **in 1909. Although the house was only four years old, its owner, the Rev. Percy Lloyd, had spent so much money on its construction that he was forced to move out and let it to another clergyman, the Rev. F. M. Meyrick-Jones.**

ABOVE The view
looking out from
beneath the gallery into
the great hall, which is
filled with Meyrick-
Jones's collection of
antique furniture. In
contrast to its eccentric
exterior, the interiors
of Home Place are
relatively conventional.

wing, and a billard room and library in the other.
This corridor originally supported an open first-
floor gallery looking down into the hall, but it was
soon found to be too draughty and was glazed in.
The interiors were generally far more conventional
than the exteriors, with plain plaster and exposed
oak timbering and little, apart from the occasional
odd angle, to distinguish them from most other
Domestic Revival houses of the early 1900s.

Prior's client in all this was a shadowy figure.
The Rev. Percy Lloyd was clearly possessed of a
hefty private income. But it wasn't hefty enough.

The eventual cost of Home Place was far in excess
of Prior's £8,000 (about $13,000) estimate.
According to some accounts, the final bill was a
colossal £60,000 ($90,000). Poor Lloyd had to
let the house, almost as soon as it was finished, to
another clergyman, the Rev. F. M. Meyrick-Jones,
who promptly imported his collection of antiques
and "objects of old domestic use in brass and
iron." How ironic and how sad that Prior's heroic
attempt to build something that broke loose from
the shackles of historical styles should be filled
with old furniture and pots and pans.

No Magic Quality

Ambrose Heal and the commercialization of craft

One of the great dilemmas — some would say *the* great dilemma — at the heart of the Arts and Crafts movement was whether or not to allow the machine a place in the creative process. Handcrafted artefacts were prohibitively expensive. In 1914, for example, four trestle tables from the Gimson–Barnsley workshops took 383 man-hours to make. A more elaborate walnut bureau took 629 man-hours, and its selling price of £51 (about $81), including only 10 percent profit to the firm, represented the entire annual income of a well-paid agricultural labourer. Yet Ruskin and Morris had taught that the mass production that would bring a chair or a table within the reach of the deserving poor (or at least the deserving lower middle-classes) also meant a lowering of standards, and broke the all-important link between creator and creation.

Technophobia was much more acute among British Arts and Crafts designers than in Europe or America. This wasn't surprising: the movement

LEFT Bow-fronted oak dressing table from Heal & Son. Ambrose Heal's biographer recalled that "his most important service to furniture-making was... to produce chastely designed and comfortable pieces which were an adornment to the home and not so expensive as to be obtainable only by the wealthy."

was born in Britain in the 1850s and 1860s out of a belief that assembly-line production and the mechanization of labour resulted in poor design and the dehumanization of the craftsman, and it was in Britain that the moral value placed on handcrafted goods was highest. Even so, in his later years, Morris himself realized that it was unrealistic to see the Industrial Revolution as a regrettable but rectifiable error; instead, he was prepared to concede, "I would do some things by machinery that are now done by hand, and other things by hand that are now done by machinery."

By the 1890s, others were becoming irritated by the simplistic division between the ideal of the artist-craftsman who designed and made an artefact, and the factories that churned out badly designed fripperies in the hundreds of thousands. Was it not possible, asked *The Studio* in 1897, for manufacturers to "submit cheap and comely furniture, well-decorated pottery for household use, dinner and tea services and the like, artistic but inexpensive table glass, cretonnes, and carpets" produced in a factory rather than a workshop?

LEFT The furniture-designer and businessman Ambrose Heal was one of the first Englishmen to overcome the Arts and Crafts movement's distaste for modern production methods. "The machine," he wrote, "relieves the workman of a good deal of drudgery, and legitimately cheapens production."

Ambrose Heal (1872–1959), of the furniture retailer Heal & Son, and a gifted designer in his own right, heeded this call, recognizing a niche in the market. Heal was the great-grandson of John Harris Heal, whose bedding business at Rathbone Place, Oxford Street, had gradually expanded to take in first bedsteads, then general furnishings. After studying at the Slade School of Art in London, Heal was apprenticed to a cabinet-maker in Warwick, where he learned the craft of furniture design before joining the family firm in 1893. Through his cousin Cecil Brewer, an architect and a member of the Art-Workers' Guild, he came into contact with the leading lights of the Arts and Crafts movement; their influence showed in his first catalogues of designs for Heal & Son: "Plain Oak Furniture," which appeared in 1898,

and "Simple Bedroom Furniture," issued the following year. The difference was that Ambrose Heal wasn't afraid of the machine. "The sawing of planks from the rough and the rough planing and smoothing of them are evidently operations which admit of no magic quality being imparted to them by the hand of the workman," he once wrote. "The machine just happens to be speedier, relieves the workman of a good deal of drudgery, and legitimately cheapens production."

Under his direction (Ambrose was managing director from 1907 and chairman from 1913), Heal & Son sold good-looking, sturdy cupboards, dressers, and sideboards in weathered oak, elm, and chestnut. This was plain, honest furniture, which declared its structure, revelled in its materials, and drew on the same seventeenth- and eighteenth-century country pieces that had inspired Morris & Co., Gimson and the Barnsleys, Voysey, and Ashbee. But at the same time, it utilized modern production methods and hence was available at realistic prices.

At first there was a good deal of opposition, not so much from Heal's high-minded fellow artists as from within his own firm. Cabinet-makers, accustomed to producing the heavily ornamented monstrosities that passed for furniture at the turn of the century, grumbled that such work was beneath them; salesmen said they couldn't be expected to sell "prison furniture." But it soon became clear that the market was there, among the thousands of earnest young couples who read Ruskin's *The Stones of Venice* and Morris's *News from Nowhere* to each other in the evenings, but who could afford to do no more than look wistfully in the shop windows of the Oxford Street art furnishers. By disentangling Arts and Crafts design from its anti-industrial roots, Ambrose Heal not only enabled people like these to fill their homes with furniture that would otherwise have been far beyond their reach; he also made the machine a servant rather than a devil, and dragged the British Arts and Crafts revolution kicking and screaming into the twentieth century.

LEFT **A light oak "Letchworth" dresser from Heal & Son. The introduction of straightforward, simple furniture like this came as a shock to the firm's cabinet-makers and sales-people, who were convinced it wouldn't sell. They were wrong.**

RODMARTON MANOR

Ernest Barnsley for Claud Biddulph, 1909–29

As far as the theorists of the Arts and Crafts movement were concerned, a house was not to be imposed on a client. It should be a meeting of minds and skills, a communal effort akin to a medieval building project, in which designer, consumer, and estate workforce collaborated to produce something that was not the individual vision of the architect-as-artist, but a collective expression of traditional values.

Not surprisingly, the times when such a high-flown ideal could be put into practice were few and far between. No matter what they might say in public, most Arts and Crafts architects resented any interference in their work. For their part, the architects' wealthy patrons usually wanted pleasant, fashionable homes. They were reluctant to pay for grandiose social experiments which, because of their emphasis on hand-crafted work and their rejection of modern construction techniques, might take years, decades even, to reach fruition.

Rodmarton Manor in Gloucestershire is unique, because here the dream was realized. That dream belonged initially to Ernest Barnsley, who had remained in Sapperton after his quarrel with Sydney Gimson, designing buildings and furniture and championing the cause of the Craft Revival. But it was soon shared by his clients, Claud Biddulph and his wife Margaret.

Claud Biddulph was given the 550-acre Rodmarton estate by his father in 1894, when he was just eighteen. There was no seat to go with it – the medieval manor house had fallen into decay in the previous century – but this didn't really matter, since as a young man Claud preferred a career in the City to life as a country squire. In 1906, however, he married; and soon afterwards he and Margaret decided to make their home at Rodmarton. They commissioned Ernest Barnsley to come up with designs for what Claud was wont to call their "cottage in the country" – half-jokingly, because for all its quiet charm and its studied references to the Cotswold vernacular,

ABOVE **As clients, Claud and Margaret Biddulph were an Arts and Crafts architect's dream – socially concerned, wealthy enough to build on a large scale, and possessing the patience and confidence to stand by and wait while their new house was constructed according to traditional methods.**

LEFT **Rodmarton Manor, Gloucestershire, was designed by Arts and Crafts architect Ernest Barnsley and completed after his death by his son-in-law, Norman Jewson. Their client, Claud Biddulph, liked to refer to this substantial, imposing house half-jokingly as his "cottage in the country."**

Rodmarton is a substantial and imposing house, all the more imposing for its sweeping gabled façade (unkindly described by *The Builder* as having "the somewhat unfortunate skyline effect of an upturned and magnified saw"), which disguises a plan that is basically only one room deep.

Barnsley produced his first designs for Rodmarton in 1909, and shortly afterwards work began on the kitchen court and domestic offices in the east wing, progressing slowly – very slowly – westwards. Although the shell was roofed by about 1912 and the Biddulphs were able to move in in 1915, the house wasn't finished until 1929, three years after Barnsley's death, when his son-in-law Norman Jewson completed the chapel in the west wing. Such a long building history is usually due either to financial constraints or to a lack of commitment on the part of the client. Not so in Rodmarton's case. At the outset Claud told Barnsley he was prepared to set aside the hefty

annual sum of £5,000 (about $8,000) over a period of years for the creation of his "cottage," and the Biddulphs' enthusiasm for the scheme grew stronger as time passed. The long gestation period was due entirely to Barnsley's insistence on traditional working practices. No contractor was employed, and all the stone and slate was quarried nearby and brought to the site by wagon, to be worked by local masons. Timber for beams and rafters was cut and seasoned on the estate; Barnsley wouldn't allow planks to be shaped with a circular saw – that smacked of an industrial process, and came between the workman and his materials. So a sawpit was constructed on site, and two men slaved away with a two-handed saw. One wonders just how much they appreciated being part of Barnsley's stand against the Machine Age. Metalwork was made by the local blacksmith, Fred Baldwin; the Rodmarton foreman, a carpenter named Alfred Wright, acted as clerk of

BELOW **The garden front, with the charming range of gables that led a reviewer in** *The Builder* **to say that Rodmarton had "the somewhat unfortunate skyline effect of an upturned and magnified saw."**

works; and the grounds were designed by Barnsley and laid out contemporaneously with the building of the house by the head gardener, William Scrubey.

The emphasis on local involvement continued inside the house, with furniture made by Alfred Wright's joiners and designed by Ernest Barnsley, his brother Sidney, and the Chalford cabinet-maker Peter Waals. Wright's workmen also produced oak panelling from drawings by the designer Alfred Powell, whose wife Louise contributed pottery and the decoration of a piano designed by Waals. Both the Powells were regular visitors to the house, as was the Labour politician Ramsay MacDonald. The main hall was often given over to craft classes in cane work, needle-work, and woodwork for the villagers, presided over by Margaret Biddulph.

There was a serious point to all this, which went far beyond a hatred of modern civilization and a utopian hankering after a mythical pre-industrial past. Rodmarton was an educational enterprise, a quiet attempt to change the world. If traditional crafts were dying out, they must be revived; and their revival depended not on city-bred reformers like Barnsley, but on people like the Biddulphs' masons and joiners, and the Rodmarton Women's Guild, who stitched the appliqué hangings. Give them the skills and the confidence to make beautiful things, and they would pass their knowledge on to others.

This was the sort of radical social adventure that the Arts and Crafts movement in general and the Cotswold group in particular had dreamed of for two decades, but never achieved. John Rothenstein, whose father William was a regular visitor to Rodmarton, once wrote that "A hundred people doing as the Biddulphs did would have gone far to transform the face of rural England." He was wrong. It would have taken more than a hundred thousand Biddulphs to turn back the tide of history. But they did make a difference, and a small corner of Gloucestershire is enriched because of what they and their architect tried to do. That can only be a cause for celebration.

LEFT **The Biddulphs became infected with Ernest Barnsley's passionate desire to revive English crafts. Villagers attended regular classes in canework, needlework, and woodwork, held in the main hall; and the Rodmarton Women's Guild produced a series of appliqué hangings for the house.**

AN INTERNATIONAL STYLE

How the Arts and Crafts movement influenced modernism

The Arts and Crafts movement was largely finished as a living architectural tradition by the end of the 1920s. When Norman Jewson completed the chapel of Rodmarton Manor in 1929, most of the greatest exponents of Arts and Crafts had either died, like Philip Webb and Norman Shaw; or, like Edwin Lutyens, had moved on to more profitable things. Others, such as C. F. A. Voysey, were steadily being marginalized by a new generation of designers. But although the drive to repackage the vernacular was disappearing in Europe, it lingered on in Britain where resistance to modernism was strongest. The best examples included the tradition of craftsmanship established by Gimson and the Barnsleys; the worst are amply represented by the 1920s and '30s cottages, complete with *faux* beams, tiny inglenooks, and weathered-oak radios, which would have made William Morris turn in his grave.

However, in a sense the Arts and Crafts movement did not die at all. It was the historian Nikolaus Pevsner who, in the 1930s, first pointed out the debt that Walter Gropius, Le Corbusier, and the other leading Modernist architects owed

BELOW **The sitting room of Charles Rennie Mackintosh's Hill House, Helensburgh. Britain's greatest exponent of Art Nouveau, and a major influence on European design, Mackintosh had roots that were closer to the English Arts and Crafts movement than its leaders would admit.**

RIGHT The Willitts House, Highland Park, Illinois, designed by Frank Lloyd Wright (1902). "Rightly used," said Wright, "the very curse machinery puts upon handicraft should...end this wearisome struggle to make things seem what they are not and never can be."

to the early Arts and Crafts movement. He argued that the design revolution that began with Ruskin and Morris was in fact more of an evolution – the start of an unbroken but ever-changing tradition that extended to the Bauhaus and beyond.

This idea might have raised eyebrows, since at the time – in Britain, at least – people were taking refuge from the machine age in the cosy quaintness to which the Arts and Crafts movement had descended, or were busy rebelling against their parents' taste, replacing Morris carpets and Sussex chairs with furniture that reflected their faith in the future. Either way, the thought that a Gordon Russell chair was an expression of Ruskinian theory, or that the futuristic lines of Mendelsohn and Chermayeff's De La Warr Pavilion at Bexhill-on-Sea was related to a Gimson cottage, would have fundamentally disturbed their outlook.

Today we are accustomed to the idea that all cultures are continuing traditions. And one can, of course, play the same linear game with the origins of the Arts and Crafts movement itself. Without Gothicists like Pugin, could there have been a Webb? Without the picturesque Gothic follies of the late eighteenth and early nineteenth centuries, could there have been a Pugin?

BELOW A hanging lamp designed by Josef Hoffmann, one of the founders of the Wiener Werkstätte. An Austrian group of Arts and Crafts workshops, the Wiener Werkstätte initially took its lead from British groups, in particular the Guild of Handicraft set up by C. R. Ashbee.

THE GLESSNER HOUSE

Henry Hobson Richardson for John J. Glessner, 1885–7

The Glessner House is a stark, forbidding fortress of a building. It stands on Chicago's South Prairie Avenue, now a rather scruffy neighbourhood, but in the late nineteenth century a fashionable residential area where the city's elite built their mansions. The house is not so much self-effacing as pathologically private, almost as though it realized one day it would need to draw strength from itself rather than from the urbane milieu that gave birth to it. It is named after John J. Glessner, an agricultural machinery executive and also a teetotaller with cultured tastes, progressive views, and an artistic wife named Frances, who moved to Prairie Avenue in 1885.

To design their new home, John and Frances Glessner chose the charismatic Boston architect Henry Hobson Richardson (1838–86), who, along with Louis Sullivan and Frank Lloyd Wright, was a member of American architecture's triumvirate of geniuses, and was one of the few architects in history to have a style named after him. Richardsonian Romanesque, an attractive combination of round-headed openings, pyramidal roofs, and broad expanses of rock-faced masonry, became popular during the 1880s, as fellow architects tried – not always successfully – to emulate what one contemporary critic defined as Richardson's "power of disposing masses, his insistence upon largeness and simplicity, his impatience of niggling, his straightforward and virile handling of his tasks..." The tone was set by what is still his most famous building, Trinity Church on Copley Square in Boston (1872), a towering, pyramidal composition of rock-faced, yellowish-grey granite with red sandstone dressings and wide, round arches – "grandeur characterized by simplicity," to use Richardson's own words.

Henry Hobson Richardson was, quite literally, a larger-than-life figure – massive and solid, like the buildings he designed. Frances Glessner, who didn't like him very much, commented on the fact that he "breathes very heavy" and said that he was the largest person she had ever seen; John Glessner reckoned Richardson's weight at around 168kg (370lbs). The architect's chronic ill health was not helped by the fact that he persistently ignored his doctors' advice about following a sensible diet and taking plenty of rest, and he died at the age of forty-seven, leaving the house still unfinished. (It was completed by the firm that took over his work in progress, Shepley, Rutan & Coolidge.)

Richardson was much taken with the English renaissance in the decorative arts, actively promoting Morris & Co. products that were then becoming available in Boston; by 1883, three stores in the city were advertising Morris wallpapers, textiles, and carpets, and the Morris & Co. stand at the Boston Foreign Fair that took place that winter led to increased interest on the East coast. But Richardson, who was every inch the celebrity architect, was too much of an egotist, perhaps, and too preoccupied with public

building – until his final years at least – to pay much attention to the Domestic Revival in British architecture inspired by Webb and Shaw. Of the seventy-seven works catalogued in 1888 by his friend and first biographer, Mariana Griswold Van Rensselaer, only twenty-four were houses, and thirteen of these were commissioned in the last three years of his life. The Glessners, on the other hand, were Arts and Crafts devotees. Frances was a more than competent amateur metalworker in her own right; she designed a number of pieces for the house. Others came from Richardson's studio, wallpapers were bought from Morris & Co., and there were ceramics by William de Morgan.

The house was commissioned in May 1885, and Richardson sketched out the preliminary designs during dinner with his clients in Chicago. That September, while the Glessners were at their summer residence in New Hampshire, they were invited to spend a couple of days with him at his house in Brookline, near Boston, to see a more detailed scheme. Richardson set out to impress, presenting them with signed photographs of himself, taking them for a tour of Trinity Church, and finally wining and dining them at his country club. Whether the Glessners impressed him is a different matter: when he dramatically unveiled his plans for their house, Frances merely commented that he hadn't provided enough closets. He abruptly discarded the drawing.

The Glessner House was built on a large corner plot, but Richardson, instead of setting it back from the street where it could invite admiration and make public claims for its owners' status, opted for an L-shaped plan that wrapped the building round the corner, with a main

BELOW **The slender balusters of the staircase provide a delicate contrast with the chunky, almost Craftsmanlike panelling. Richardson was hailed in his day as one of the first American architects to concern himself with every detail.**

RIGHT The Prairie
Avenue entrance to
the house manages
to combine echoes of
the Romanesque with
a severe simplicity that
refuses to proclaim its
owners' status, while
at the same time
suggesting a sense of
privacy that carefully
excludes the outsider
from the warm interiors
which lie beyond.

The life of the house took place on the first floor, where the usual domestic offices — butler's pantry, kitchen, servants' hall, and storerooms — adjoined the stable block, with a long, narrow service corridor running down the street side, sheltering the well-lit family rooms which looked out into the courtyard. The D-shaped dining room, which projected out into the court, adjoined the butler's pantry. Next to this was the parlour, and then the hall, a glorious curved space tucked into the angle of the L, with the library nestling in behind it. First-floor accommodation was completed by a master bedroom with dressing rooms and a bathroom extending out over the carriage drive.

The contrast between public façade and private space strikes one most forcibly in the Glessner House — that, and the warm, opulent gleam of the panelled interiors and the disconcerting Englishness of the Morris wallcoverings, which are perhaps all part of the same thing. "Richardson's last houses were distinctly his best," wrote Van Rensselaer, "and we may believe that had he lived a few years longer he would have improved even upon these." That's something we'll never know: but in his emphasis on the sanctity of domesticity, Richardson unwittingly showed a sympathy with his contemporaries in the British Arts and Crafts movement. In his ability to adapt historical styles without descending into mere historicism, he proved that residential architecture in the United States had come of age.

entrance and carriage drive on the short arm of the L and an enclosed courtyard behind it. All the house's excitement which, with its projecting round and polygonal towers, sweeping external stairs, and broad horizontal bands of masonry, is considerable, was confined to this courtyard. The house belonged exclusively to the Glessners, rather than to casual passers-by, who had to content themselves with an entrance arch within a rather severe façade on Prairie Avenue, and an even more severe stone wall around the corner on the long arm of the L, only punctuated by the small round arch of the servants' doorway and a wider opening leading to the connecting stable block. This was deliberate. Two years after Richardson's death, Van Rensselaer recalled that the design for the Glessner House had given him "peculiar satisfaction." The architect, she said, "considered the scheme fortunate both as affording a retirement not often secured in our city dwellings, and as allowing him to build on the side street one of those plain massive walls in which he always delighted."

Richardson may have delighted in plain massive walls, but the Glessners' neighbours, used to their own brand of showy beaux-arts classicism, were disconcerted by the house's austerity. In fact they hated it, although the Glessners were thrilled: Frances later described it as "truly beautiful and in every way desirable and delightful."

BELOW Fireplace detail. The interiors of the Glessner House present a warm synthesis of its owners' "advanced" artistic tastes and Richardson's prediliction for gentlemen's club opulence.

INTERNATIONAL EXHIBITIONS

How the Arts and Crafts movement was spread abroad

William Morris learned early on the commercial sense of maintaining a presence at the international expositions that were held in Europe and the United States with bewildering frequency during the second half of the nineteenth century. It was, after all, the 1862 International Exhibition at South Kensington in London that launched Morris, Marshall, Faulkner & Co. Others followed Morris's example. The architect and designer E. W. Godwin, for instance, had great success when he showed his furniture at the 1876 Centennial Exhibition in Philadelphia. So did Morris & Co., when the company took space at the 1883–4 Foreign Fair in Boston. They exhibited 1,350 square feet of curtains, carpets, damasks, and velvets, hand-printed cottons, wallpapers, tapestries, embroideries, two stained-glass windows designed by Edward Burne-Jones, and even a selection of dress-silks. "It may be thought strange," said manager George Wardle in the Firm's guide to the exhibits, "that Mr. Morris should concern himself with the colours of ladies' dresses... [but] in England the calls upon him to provide something that ladies might wear in rooms he had helped to make lovely, were too many to be disregarded."

However, when Walter Crane (1845–1915) and fellow-members of the Art Workers' Guild first planned an exhibition – originally titled "The Combined Arts," but changed to "Arts and Crafts" before the show opened – Morris poured cold water on the idea, declaring that "the general public don't care one damn about the arts and crafts; and our customers can come to our shops to look at our kind of goods." But he came round to the idea by the time the Arts and Crafts Exhibition Society's first venture opened on October 4, 1888. In fact, not only were plenty of the Firm's products on display, but at later exhibitions Morris himself gave lectures, and even a demonstration of weaving.

Public reaction to the Society's shows was generally enthusiastic. Commenting on the first, *The Builder* thought it showed "what real progress has been made in decorative design during the last quarter of a century"; while in a review (for an American journal) of the third in 1890, a young W. B. Yeats said that "'but for these 'arts and crafts' exhibitions...the outer public would hardly be able to judge of the immense change

ABOVE **Walter Crane, illustrator, designer, socialist, and one of the leading figures behind the formation of the Arts and Crafts Exhibition Society. Crane's mission, as he wrote in the catalogue to the Society's first exhibition in 1888, was "to turn our artists into craftsmen and our craftsmen into artists."**

LEFT **An Anglo-Japanese wing cabinet in red hardwood with brass fittings, designed by E. W. Godwin. The piece was bought by a wealthy Philadelphia collector named Arthur Biddle. According to family tradition, it was purchased after the Biddles saw Godwin's work on show at the Philadelphia Centennial Exposition of 1876.**

RIGHT The interior of the American Bar in Vienna, designed by the greatest theorist of the Modern movement, Adolph Loos (1870–1933). In spite of their desire to break with past styles, the Modernists nevertheless acknowledged their debt to the English Arts and Crafts movement.

that is going on in all kinds of decorative art." *The Magazine of Art*, on the other hand, observed rather snootily that "over all there hovers an air of galvanised mediaevalism; the tendency is rather to resuscitate or imitate than to originate."

Although the Arts and Crafts Exhibition Society tended to be quite insular, the same could not be said of the movement's followers from continental Europe. In Brussels, the group of avant-garde artists who called themselves Les Vingt ("The Twenty") included the decorative arts in their exhibitions during the 1890s; in 1894 they invited contributions from Morris & Co., the

Kelmscott Press, and C. R. Ashbee. Morris & Co. and Ashbee also exhibited at Liège the following year, along with Burne-Jones and Walter Crane; and the work of Ashbee (again), Charles Rennie Mackintosh, and Margaret Macdonald was featured at the Vienna Secession exhibition of 1900. European artists and designers, still eager to learn from Britain, shared the sentiments of Josef Hoffmann, one of the founders of the Secession: "Our aim is to create an island of tranquillity in our own country, which, amid the joyful hum of arts and crafts, would be welcome to anyone who professes faith in Ruskin and Morris."

HILL HOUSE

Charles Rennie Mackintosh for Walter W. Blackie, 1902–4

The builder of Hill House was a man of pronounced architectural tastes. Glasgow publisher Walter W. Blackie (1860–1953) did not like red-tiled roofs; he did not want an Old English construction of brick, plaster, and wooden beams; he did want grey roughcast walls and slates; and he was firmly of the opinion that any desired architectural effect should be secured by the massing of the parts rather than by adventitious ornament. He was particularly fortunate, then, in his choice of architect.

Charles Rennie Mackintosh (1868–1928) shared Blackie's distaste for the ordinary and the inappropriate, characterizing his outlook on architecture as "modern ideas in modern dress" and "designs by living men for living men."

Mackintosh's story is well known: In 1889, after studying at the Glasgow School of Art, he joined the building firm of Honeyman and Keppie, where he met and befriended Herbert MacNair. He and MacNair married two sisters, Margaret and Frances MacDonald, and "the Four," as they became known, achieved a degree of

BELOW **Hill House, Upper Helensburgh (1902–4). The south façade, showing the traditional drum turret nestling between the domestic wing to the right, and the Blackies' reception rooms to the left. The little round structure to the front, a deliberate echo of the staircase tower behind it, is a garden store.**

RIGHT Walter W. Blackie, painted in 1928 by the Glasgow artist Hilary Strain. Blackie's daughters recalled that their mother and father did not think Hill House was particularly avant-garde: "They just wanted to break away from Victorian heaviness with its double curtains, patterned wallpaper, and elaborate furniture."

important influence on Mackintosh's early career, used to refer to the Four dismissively as the "Spook School"; Arts and Crafts designers were profoundly distrustful of what, in another context, May Morris called "a hair-shirt vigour... opposed to all geniality or prandial humours"; and the English architectural establishment in general thought the Beardsleyesque curves and mannered geometrical forms of Mackintosh's designs to be decadent, unwholesome, and dangerously precious. (This was, after all, in the wake of the Oscar Wilde trial of 1895, when artistic tendencies were regarded as unmanly, Beardsley's books were withdrawn from railway bookstalls, and young dandies all over England grew beards and took to wearing tweeds.)

However, it was exactly these "unwholesome" qualities that appealed to the European artists who saw and admired Mackintosh's work in Munich and Liège, at the Vienna Secession in 1900, or at the 1902 Turin International Exhibition of Modern Decorative Art. Friedrich Ahler-Hestermann remembered forty years later how Viennese designers, already bored with the "eternal solid goodness of English interiors," were enthralled at the sight of "spaces containing nothing but two straight chairs on a white carpet, looking silently and spectrally at each other across a little table, and by rooms like dreams, narrow panels, grey silk, very very slender wooden shafts — verticals everywhere." Muthesius lauded Mackintosh as "a genius...[marking] the way to excellence for mankind in the future," and sent him boxes of liqueur chocolates.

Blackie's fears that "so distinguished a performer would be too big a man for me" were soon overcome. At their first meeting, when the publisher laid down his architectural likes and dislikes, he found that Mackintosh readily agreed with them all. A visit was arranged to Windyhill, a house the young architect had just built and furnished at Kilmacolm for the businessman and art collector William Davidson. Windyhill is plain, even severe — Davidson's friends used to joke that it looked like a prison or a barracks — but Mr and Mrs Blackie liked what they saw and left "convinced that Mackintosh was the man for us."

fame (and some notoriety) for their pioneering Art Nouveau designs, which rejected academic traditions and drew loosely on ancient Celtic ornament. In 1913, full of drink and disillusionment, Mackintosh resigned his partnership with Honeyman and Keppie and left Scotland forever, dying of cancer in London fifteen years later.

It was Mackintosh's most prominent building, the Glasgow School of Art (1897–9; 1907–9), that in a roundabout way led to his meeting with Walter Blackie. In the spring of 1902, the Blackie family decided to move from their Dunblane home. They acquired a site in Upper Helensburgh looking down to the Firth of Clyde, some twenty miles north-west of Glasgow but still within easy reach of Blackie's office in the city by rail. The east wing of the School of Art had recently been completed, and Blackie had followed its progress with a mildly proprietorial interest: his late uncle, Robert Blackie, had been a leading figure in Scottish artistic circles and a member of the board of governors at the school. Walter Blackie asked his art director, Talwin Morris, who was responsible for the building. Morris told him it was Mackintosh and suggested this was just the man to design his boss's new home.

Initially, Blackie was hesitant about asking for a design from such a prominent figure. In spite of Mackintosh's later protestations that he never received the recognition due to him, by 1902 he was respected in Scotland and positively feted in continental Europe — although not, admittedly, in England. Voysey, whose buildings were an

Hill House was finished around the end of 1903, and the family moved there in March 1904. According to Blackie, Mackintosh handed

over the house to them and said: "Here is the house. It is not an Italian villa, an English mansion house, a Swiss chalet, or a Scotch castle. It is a dwelling house." Given the architect's determination to break free from a dependence on historical styles, the claim is understandable, but a shade disingenuous: Hill House owes more to historical precedent than he was prepared to admit. Yes, Blackie was granted his roughcast walls and slate roofs, his effective massing of parts, and there was no hint of picturesque Old-

English quaintness nor any adventitious ornament. But for all its austere modernity, Hill House has about it a good dash of Scotch castle or, more accurately, of the tower-houses prevalent in Scotland in the seventeeth and eighteenth centuries. The old historic Scottish forms resonate through the sheer walls of the exterior, showing themselves not only in more obvious details such as the drum staircase turret tucked into the angle between the dining room and the block containing domestic offices, the

ABOVE **The Blackies' bedroom, with stylized stencilled roses, a Mackintosh ladderback chair, and, on the far right, a washstand with leaded mirror also designed by Mackintosh. The architect drew a plan of the bedroom showing exactly where to stand each item of furniture.**

childrens' nurseries, and the schoolroom, but in the building's powerful vertical emphasis and sparse, asymmetrical fenestration.

"Scottish Baronial architecture," he once said, "is a subject dear to my heart and entwined among my inmost thoughts and affections...I only hope that [its revival] will not be strangled in its infancy by indiscriminate and unsympathetic people who copy the ancient examples without trying to make it conform to modern requirements." Step inside Hill House, and any thoughts of Mackintosh as a slavish copyist are banished in an instant. Although he took a hand in many of the details of the interiors, from cupboards and clothes presses to fireplace accessories, the four rooms to which he paid special attention were the long, narrow, entrance hall, which was single-storeyed in a deliberate break with the usual Edwardian country house convention; the library beside it; the drawing-room on the south side of the house, looking out over the garden; and the Blackies' master bedroom, on the first floor. Not surprisingly, these spaces show Mackintosh at his best. They are filled with bold geometrical forms that refuse to acknowledge any historical precedent. Light fittings are decorated in daring abstract patterns. Stencilled roses are reduced to unnatural, stylized forms. Soft white walls contrast with the ebonized black of impossibly elongated ladderback chairs. A shallow drawing-room inglenook with two tiny seats reduced to little more than perches, laughs in the face of the cosy domestic virtues espoused by Webb, Shaw, Lutyens, and Voysey.

Mackintosh's relationship with English Arts and Crafts theory is a complicated one. From Voysey, he borrowed clean lines and simplicity, as well as specific details such as the tapered chimneystacks and massive, unbroken wall-surfaces of Hill House — although in this last he was also influenced by Baillie Scott, whose carefully unhistoricist White House at Helensburgh (1899) he must have seen during site visits to the Blackies' house. More generally, he took the Arts and Crafts movement's beliefs in the appropriateness of vernacular architecture and regional contextualism, its preoccupation with design as high art, and its growing conviction that the architect/designer should be responsible for every last detail. "Architecture is

the world of art," he said, "and as it is everything visible and invisible that makes the world, so it is all the arts and crafts and industries that make architecture." In practice, however, Mackintosh was supremely indifferent to the obsession of those in the English Arts and Crafts movement with good, honest construction; his furniture is notorious for being not only badly made but also morally suspect for carefully concealing its true structure. However, he can be forgiven this for the shining beauty of the Hill House interiors. Indeed, if there is a fault with those interiors, it is that they are too designerly, too artistic. In breaking with the easy domesticity of the Morrisites, he created spaces that were stunning to look at but difficult to live in. "Even a book in an unsuitable binding would disturb the atmosphere simply by lying on the table," said Muthesius, and he was one of Mackintosh's biggest fans. Eighty years after Hill House was completed, Blackie's daughters recalled a childhood memory of an incident that could come straight from a play by Oscar Wilde. Their mother had placed some yellow flowers in the entrance hall, with its greys, blues, pinks, and blacks. When he saw them, Mackintosh made a tremendous fuss: they would ruin his colour-scheme, he said. Mrs Blackie moved the flowers.

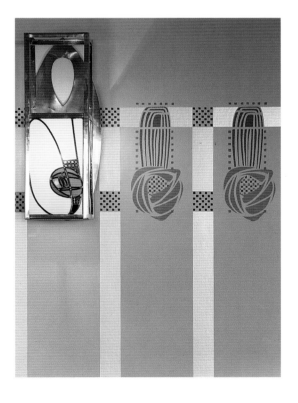

RIGHT Light fitting and stencilled hanging roses in the drawing-room. The natural forms that Morris had rehabilitated in his textiles and wallpaper designs back in the 1860s and 1870s have been reduced almost to abstractions in this design.

THE ART NOUVEAU MOVEMENT

"That strange decorative disease known as L'Art Nouveau," as Walter Crane once described it, swept through much of Europe in the 1890s. With its whiplash curves, exaggerated organic forms, and what has been described as its ultimate motif, the rhythmic contorted line that throbs with a sense of movement, Art Nouveau made its presence felt in all branches of the visual and applied arts, from architecture, painting, and graphic design to furniture, jewellery, glassware, and metalwork.

The style takes its name from a gallery, the Maison de l'Art Nouveau, which opened in Paris in December 1895. Its proprietor, a dealer named

Samuel Bing, recalled six years later that he had never intended to proclaim the start of a new artistic movement, but simply to provide a meeting ground "for all ardent young spirits anxious to show the modernity of their tendencies." The fact that his first exhibition showed work by Crane, Rodin, and Pissarro along with glass by Tiffany and Gallé, furniture by Henry van de Velde, and prints by Aubrey Beardsley suggests that Bing did not have any developed artistic programme in mind, but simply wanted to show new art.

However, when the Maison de l'Art Nouveau opened, the distinctive style was already growing steadily in importance. One of its earliest pioneers

BELOW **Gloriously extravagant ornament on the entrance façade of the Atelier Elvira in Munich, a photographer's studio designed by the architect August Endell in 1897–8. The daring design of the building proved too much for the Nazis, who decided that it reflected alarmingly degenerate tendencies, and ordered it to be pulled down.**

architect August Endell (1871–1925), whose stunning Atelier Elvira in Munich (1897–8) was considered degenerate by the Nazis and demolished, the movement was called Jugendstil, after the decorative arts magazine *Jugend*. In Italy, curiously, it was called Stile Liberty, after the London store that specialized in Art Nouveau textiles, and in Spain it was known as Modernisme.

Indeed, Spain produced the greatest and most outrageous of the Art Nouveau architects – Antoni Gaudí (1852–1926), who worked in and around Barcelona. Gaudi's most famous work is the Church of the Sagrada Familia (1883–1926, see page 156), in which he gradually moved from a relatively orthodox Gothic Revivalism to ever more bizarre and fantastic shapes. Spiky towers, encrusted with twisting ornament, pierced through at every opportunity, and sprouting curious berry-like globules, turn the church into a Disneyland castle – except that nowhere in Disneyland can you find anything so far removed from reality.

Many of the leading European Art Nouveau designers had links with, or at least a sound knowledge of and respect for, the English Arts and Crafts movement, but that respect was not reciprocated. The work of Charles Rennie Mackintosh – the closest thing Britain had to an Art Nouveau architect – was rejected as unwholesome by his English contemporaries. The other great home-grown talent was the illustrator Aubrey Beardsley, who worked on two particularly "advanced" magazines: the quarterly *Yellow Book*, which ran from 1894 until 1897 (although Beardsley was forced to resign as art editor after the Wilde trial, because he was found guilty of

ABOVE **Karlsplatz Underground Station in Vienna, designed in 1898–9 by Otto Wagner (1841–1918). For a time in the 1890s Wagner was an influential exponent of Art Nouveau in Austria, although his respect for structural principles soon led him to call for a more functional simplicity in architecture.**

was the Belgian Victor Horta (1861–1947), whose first major buildings, the Hôtel Autrique (1893–5) and the Hôtel Tassel (1893–7), both in Brussels, already showed all the characteristic features of the style: swirling curvilinear tendrils creep across walls, lie embedded in mosaic floors, and rise up to the ceiling in iron balustrades and brackets. His own house and studio, the slightly later Maison and Atelier Horta (1898–1901, also in Brussels), is a triumph of form over function, and one of the movement's great landmarks.

In the later 1890s the most notable Art Nouveau products were French: the métro stations of Hector Guimard (1867–1942), who modestly suggested the name "Style Guimard"; the style, textiles, furniture, and porcelain of Georges de Feure (1868–1943); the early glassware and jewellery of René Lalique (1860–1945); and the posters by Czech-born Alphonse Mucha (1860–1939) for Bières de la Meuse and Moët & Chandon. However, the style soon appeared in different guises all over Europe. In Vienna, it was associated with the Secession. In Germany, where one of its most prominent exponents was the

RIGHT **Decorative panel on a mahogany vitrine designed by Hector Guimard (*c*.1900). Best known for his elaborate entrances to the Paris Métro (1899–1904), Guimard's furniture and interior decoration was described by an English contemporary as "fit only for cannibals."**

illustrating an edition of Wilde's *Salome*), and the short-lived *Savoy* (1895–6). Beardsley himself was also short-lived, and perhaps if he had not died of consumption in 1898, at the tragically young age of twenty-six, the style might have had a greater impact on British design. But perhaps not. His sinister black-and-white illustrations and his schoolboyish obsession with genitalia can have done little to reassure the earnest Morrisites, and his posthumous reputation was not helped by the fact that although "in my death agony," he begged his publisher, Leonard Smithers to destroy all his obscene drawings. Smithers not only failed to comply with this last request, he reissued them, even paying an impoverished barrister in the Inner Temple to forge dozens more.

By and large, Britain rejected Art Nouveau. One critic stated that "it was not the sort of thing that a clean and manly nature could thrive upon." Another, writing in *The Studio*, dismissed Gallé's glassware as "barbarous...clumsy and pretentious in conception and realisation alike," and condemned an interior by Hector Guimard as "fit only for cannibals – nothing more ugly, more pretentious or more inartistic could be conceived; one shudders at the idea of being condemned to live amid horrors such as these." It is tempting to see in all this vitriol little more than an expression of traditional English virtues, such as xenophobia and a sublime lack of imagination, and no doubt there were elements of these. But it went much deeper, particularly where the Arts and Crafts movement was concerned. The sensuality of "the Squirm," as the movement was contemptuously called, was suspect and upsetting: C. F. A. Voysey declared it to be "distinctly unhealthy and revolting...not worthy to be called a style." He went on to ask: "Is it not merely the work of a lot of imitators with nothing but mad eccentricity as a guide; good men, no doubt, misled into thinking that art is a debauch of sensuous feeling, instead of the expression of human thought and feeling combined and governed by reverence for something higher than human nature?"

Not surprisingly, English Arts and Crafts architects and designers mistrusted Art Nouveau's lack of a Ruskinian ideology, the fact that it was all surface and no purpose – style without moral content. They mistrusted the way in which it seemed to spurn the use of traditional motifs and honest constructional techniques: the curvilinear distortions of natural shapes, applied to everything from advertising posters to glass vases, from metal chandeliers to whole buildings, seemed frivolous to such serious-minded socialists as W. R. Lethaby and Philip Webb. Most of all, however, they mistrusted the newness of Art Nouveau. It had no grounding in the past, they said, and without that, it could not last.

As it happens, they were right. By the early years of the twentieth century, the tremendous vitality that was always at the very heart of Art Nouveau was already starting to flag, weighed down by an avalanche of cheap imitations. Ironically, what Art Nouveau's sternest critics within the Arts and Crafts movement failed to see was that by their insularity and their inability to respond positively to new trends in design, they were sowing the seeds of their own downfall.

RIGHT **Stained glass and sinuous curves in the top-lit staircase of the Maison and Atelier Horta on the rue Americaine in Brussels (1898–1901).**

ABOVE **Detail of the Maison Horta staircase. The writhing, contorted lines, at once tense and fluid, serve no purpose whatsoever except to express a joy in creation. One of Art Nouveau's finest interiors, the Maison Horta was extensively restored in the 1990s and now houses the Musée Horta.**

LEFT **More Disneyland than Disneyland itself: the transept of the fantastic and still unfinished Church of the Sagrada Familia in Barcelona by Antoni Gaudí (1883–1926). The historian Nikolaus Pevsner believed that Gaudí was "the only genius produced by the Art Nouveau."**

LAVEROCKDALE

Robert Stodart Lorimer, 1912–14

In 1904, the architect Hermann Muthesius reckoned that "the great movement that began in England in the 1860s and drew with such good results on earlier vernacular styles of building found no response in Scotland." He went on to say that Morris's work was unknown north of the border, and later Arts and Crafts architecture did not arrive until it had been taken up and modified by Continental exponents; and even then, it spread only to a very limited extent.

Muthesius singled out the work of just one Scottish architect as an exception to what he saw as a lamentable state of affairs. The only true representative of the English Arts and Crafts movement in Scotland, he said, the first to recognise the charm of unpretentious old Scottish buildings with their "honest plainness and simple, almost rugged massiveness," was the Edinburgh-born Robert Stodart Lorimer (1864–1929), who was to design Laverockdale, just to the south-west of his birthplace. As far as Muthesius was concerned, Lorimer was single-handedly doing for Scotland what Richard Norman Shaw and Philip Webb had done for England in the 1860s; and it was in Lorimer that Scotland's hopes for a domestic revival lay: "Scotland will not achieve what England has already achieved – a completely national style of house-building based on the old

BELOW "Simple, almost rugged massiveness": Laverockdale, near Edinburgh, was one of twenty or so cottages, villas, and mansions in the fashionable suburb of Colinton that were designed by the architect R. S. Lorimer around the turn of the century.

ABOVE Sir Robert Stodart Lorimer and friend. A brilliant interpreter of Scottish vernacular, Lorimer was described in 1904 as "the only true representative" of the Arts and Crafts movement in Scotland.

vernacular architecture — until it follows the lead given by Lorimer." In bemoaning Scotland's apparent rejection of Arts and Crafts vernacular, Muthesius was implicitly denying any connection between that movement and the work of Mackintosh and his circle. (This isn't surprising — the English did exactly the same thing. The Arts and Crafts Exhibition Society, for example, gave the Glasgow Group a rocky reception when they exhibited at its 1896 triennial show in London.) Muthesius was mistaken in his assumption, but his estimation of Lorimer as Scotland's heir to the Webb-Shaw tradition was perceptive and accurate.

Lorimer is often described as "the Scottish Lutyens," and there are parallels between the two, although the epithet somehow makes him sound derivative and second-rate — which he was not. Like his English contemporary, he developed a thriving country house practice which was tirelessly promoted by *Country Life*. Like Lutyens, he gained official honours for his services to architecture: his knighthood came in 1911 (seven years before Lutyens received his) for his work on the Gothic Thistle Chapel at St Giles's Cathedral, Edinburgh; and in 1928 he was made a Knight of the British Empire in recognition of his designs for the Scottish National War Memorial at Edinburgh Castle. And also like Lutyens, Lorimer in later life developed a penchant for the grandiose and monumental.

But Lorimer's relationship with the Arts and Crafts movement was more lasting and, in many ways, more thoughtful than that of Lutyens. Lorimer trained with the Edinburgh architect R. Rowand Anderson and then in London with the rather more exciting, muscular Gothicist G. F. Bodley. But after meeting with William Morris in 1889, he began to adopt a more thoroughgoing Arts and Crafts approach to architecture. Although he returned to Edinburgh, setting up his own practice there four years later, he continued to maintain his links with members of the movement in London, regularly exhibiting furniture designs at the Arts and Crafts Society triennials, and in 1896 he became a member of

the Art Workers' Guild. Lorimer began to attract national attention with his sensitive restoration of Earlshall, Fife (1893–4), a sixteenth-century tower house owned by R. W. Mackenzie, a friend of his parents. He managed to retain the robust, historic character of the building without descending into the prevalent florid Scottish Baronial style, and turned it into a comfortable home. He also laid out attractive formal gardens and devised the furniture (much of it in a Scots Renaissance style), which was produced, in true Arts and Crafts tradition, by local craftspeople. The village joiner, for example, made up dressers and chests for the house.

Laverockdale (1912–14) is a good example of Lorimer's mature style, which, in an extensive practice that extended both north and south of the border and encompassed churches, monuments, restorations such as the medieval Lympne Castle in Kent (1906–12), and new country houses and villas (Ardkinglas, Argyll, 1906; Formakin, Renfrewshire, 1912–14), was

RIGHT **Austere and unpretentious, Laverockdale evokes and reinterprets traditional Scottish vernacular forms from the seventeenth and eighteenth centuries, placing them in a prosperous bourgeois setting, while resisting the temptation to proclaim its occupants' status.**

notable for the tact and sophistication with which he responded to local cultural conventions. Laverockdale itself exemplifies Lorimer's comfortable adaptation of traditional Scottish forms. It stands in Colinton, once an industrial area with paper mills and grain mills, which had become an exclusive Edinburgh suburb. By 1895 Colinton was being described as having recently changed "for the better, a good many comfortable, old-English-looking houses having arisen upon its upper outskirts."

This was due in part to architects such as Lorimer's old employer, Rowand Anderson, who settled there in the early 1880s and built a series of villas with half-timbered brick gables and roughcast walls; but Colinton's subsequent architectural character is largely Lorimer's creation. In 1893, while still working on the restoration of Earlshall, he designed a "cottage" on Pentland Avenue — actually more of a substantial middle-class villa. Rough-cast and red-tiled with a round turret, Colinton Cottage showed a healthy and, for its time, quite progressive respect for native Scottish precedent, attracting attention in the English architectural press and leading to a string of commissions in the neighbourhood.

Between 1893 and 1914 Lorimer designed around twenty houses in Colinton, ranging from small, white rough-cast cottages to large, gabled and turreted villas. Laverockdale is the biggest, and one of the last. It is a peculiarly pleasing composition of rubble walls and stone-slated roofs, conjuring up images of seventeenth-century Scotland with its gables and little sash windows. It is austere certainly, with the same hard, northern resilience that Lethaby evoked at Melsetter (see page 34), the same determined verticality that Mackintosh employed at Hill House (see page 150). But it has none of Melsetter's feyness, none of Mackintosh's stylized exaggerations. Like the best English Arts and Crafts houses, Laverockdale pleases not because it stands out, but because it doesn't. It shows Robert Lorimer at his best — not as a "Scottish Lutyens," but as Lorimer.

LEFT **This rather bizarre photograph of a Laverockdale interior shows oriental wall-hangings looking out on a children's playroom, complete with climbing rope, swing, see-saw, and hobby-horse. Did Lorimer really envisage that anyone would swing from a trapeze in his puritanical suburban mansion?**

THE STORER HOUSE

Frank Lloyd Wright for Dr John Storer, 1923

Philip Webb and Frank Lloyd Wright are the only two architects who each have two houses represented in this book. Webb's presence needs no explanation, no excuse. As far as the early Arts and Crafts movement is concerned – in fact, as far as Victorian architecture as a whole is concerned – he towers above his contemporaries, a self-effacing genius whose houses define the Domestic Revival in England.

Wright needs a little more explanation. He was also a genius: that goes without saying. (Although it also goes without saying that he was far from self-effacing.) However, his links with the Arts and Crafts movement are at once more ambiguous than Webb's, in that while the latter's heart and soul remained with the movement for the whole of his career, Wright took what he could and then moved on. Moreover, the decision to discuss two of Wright's California homes from the 1920s – Hollyhock House (see page 88) and the Storer House – rather than earlier, more obviously Arts and Crafts-inspired buildings such as the homes he built in Oak Park, Illinois, at the beginning of his career, seems odd, even perverse, in a book on the Arts and Crafts house.

I have to confess that the reason is partly personal. As far as British readers are concerned, at least, the California houses that Wright built in his mid-fifties, sandwiched as they are between the Prairie architecture of the turn of the century and the iconic Fallingwater, built between 1935 and 1939, are neglected masterpieces, works that deserve a greater airing. However, they also show Wright learning from the past without being bound by it, not being afraid to experiment, looking for new designs for living, and, in so doing, shrugging off the deep Arts and Crafts obsession with homespun history.

The Storer House on Hollywood Boulevard is a case in point. It was the second of four homes that Wright designed in 1923 in the Los Angeles area using textile blocks. "We would take that despised outcast of the building industry – the concrete block," he said, "out from underfoot or from the gutter – find a hitherto unsuspected soul in it – make it a thing of beauty – textured like the trees." Known at the time as "knit-block" construction, the method involved pouring concrete into moulds to make precast blocks, each approximately 10cm (4in) thick. The blocks were then put in place, without the use of mortar, and steel rods were inserted horizontally and vertically to bind them together. External and internal skins, facing away from each other to create an unusual degree of unity between exterior and interior, were also knitted together by steel rods, and separated by a cavity that provided insulation.

The construction is straightforward enough, the interest of the resulting wall surfaces comes not only from the massing of elements and the advancing and receding planes, but from the texture provided by the repeating patterns of the blocks. And what textures he created. As Kenneth Frampton pointed out in his introduction to *Frank Lloyd Wright: Collected Writings: 1931–1939*, Wright conceived of himself "as a weaver rather than a sculptor and...woven fabric would be the metaphor for all of his architecture."

In the first of Wright's textile-block houses, the Millard residence in Pasadena (often known as "La Miniatura"), the architect employed a stylized cruciform design. The Samuel Freeman House used plain and patterned blocks, with the patterns usually paired to mirror each other, while the last and most monumental of the quartet, the Ennis House on Glendower Avenue, is a futuristic fortress of a house, looking strangely reminiscent of an early set from the sci-fi television series *Star Trek*, with the vaguely Mayan blocks sometimes

RIGHT **The exterior of the Storer House on Hollywood Boulevard, one of four "textile-block" houses designed by Frank Lloyd Wright in 1923. A mixture of plain, pierced, and textured precast concrete blocks, softened with sensitive planting and projecting at different levels, suggests an explicit rejection of traditional forms.**

RIGHT The living room of the Storer House. The almost relentless vertical banding is broken by shafts of sun from the tall windows, and by the horizontal wooden beams that span the ceiling.

LEFT The entrance to the house. Fierce geometry and severe concrete, relieved only by the glint of sunlight through the pierced blockwork, turns the experience of entering the Storer House into the discovery of some ancient American tomb.

mirror-paired, sometimes given the same orientation, and sometimes halved and separated from each other by plain concrete.

The Storer House, built for Dr John Storer, makes use of a range of different textures. There are plain blocks, blocks pierced in a Celtic cross design, and blocks with tripartite horizontal ridges, single vertical rectangles, and concentric squares. The building operates on a variety of different stepped levels, with terraces, walkways, and roof gardens. As with Hollyhock House and the other textile-block houses — all of which make use of strong horizontal and vertical grids without sloping lines or curves — the effect is ambiguously alien, partly meso-American, partly a deliberate rejection of existing Eurocentric architectural forms: wholly Frank Lloyd Wright.

The house is organized around a T-shaped plan set into a hillside, with a square kitchen, a pantry, and a servant's room leading off symmetrically to one side of the foot of the T. The core of the building is the dining room, which occupies the upright of the T and is flanked on both of its long sides by banks of vertical windows punctuated and supported by columns of blocks like the bars of a prison cage. Both here and in the living room on the second level, the ceilings are supported by exposed wooden beams, slightly incongruous memories of an earlier time.

Wright's son, Lloyd Wright, worked closely with his father on the execution of the Storer design. Although "closely" is perhaps not quite the right word for someone so completely overshadowed by his father's monumental ego, which could never be satisfied with anything that anyone else, including his own son, created. "I've just come from the Storer House," Wright wrote to him at one point. "It's a tragedy from my standpoint, but I can see how hard you've worked to pull it out and I approve many things you did." This was about as close to praise as Wright got. In the 1980s the house was restored by the Hollywood producer Joel Silver, who worked with Eric Lloyd Wright to restore the home to its original condition.

THE END OF
THE MOVEMENT

Although some of the Arts and Crafts movement's greatest architectural achievements still lay in the future, by the early 1900s critics were starting to feel disquiet at the way in which it appeared to be losing touch with its original aims. In 1906, just a decade after William Morris's death, *The Studio* reviewed the new Arts and Crafts Exhibition Society show: "The arts and crafts in this exhibition, almost failing to contend for improvement in the practical necessities of domestic comfort, have taken very seriously the covers of the books we shall read, and jewellery that will be worn in the evening." And *The Studio* had a point: exactly what contribution did enamelled brooches and tooled leather bindings make to the quality of everyday life for the masses?

Radical in its youth, the British Arts and Crafts movement grew increasingly conservative in middle age. Born out of reaction, it became reactionary, fighting a rearguard action against the spirit of the times. And during the first decades of the twentieth century it found itself politically and architecturally outflanked. The right may have thought its buildings charming, but it disapproved of the socialistic tendencies that came with them. On the left, where the struggle to improve workers' conditions was focused firmly on the organisation of labour within industry, the happy agrarian paradise foretold in Morris's *News From Nowhere* seemed simply irrelevant. In Britain the Arts and Crafts was condemned by the Labour Party as "pale and anaemic," and in truth, the movement's gentle and rather endearing Utopianism did seem somewhat wishy-washy in an age of strikes and lock-outs, scabs and militancy. Moreover, the contradictions at the heart of Morrisite ideology were becoming increasingly hard to ignore. Making expensive furniture and building big houses for bourgeois businessmen never had sat very well with

revolutionary socialism. Morris himself, through the sheer force of his charismatic personality, could just about get away with preaching the dictatorship of the proletariat one minute and counting the considerable profits he made as a capitalist entrepreneur the next. But Morris was gone, and with his passing, people began to ask just how a handmade oak dresser by Barnsley or an expensive waggon-back bed was supposed to improve the lot of the ordinary worker. And what was so ennobling about making things without the aid of machines, anyway? As H. G. Wells remarked so tellingly, apropos the house C. F. A. Voysey built for him at Sandgate in Kent in 1899: "It is a house built by hands — and some I saw were bleeding hands."

In architecture, the essentially conservative position that the British Arts and Crafts found itself trying to maintain was completely overshadowed by the work of neo-Georgians and Wrennaissance architects, led first by Richard Norman Shaw and then, after his death in 1912, by establishment figures such as Reginald Blomfield (1856–1942) and Edwin Lutyens. All three men had spent the early parts of their careers designing houses that were firmly within the Arts and Crafts tradition (and Shaw, of course, had played a pivotal part in founding that tradition); but all three moved on, firmly refusing to be bound by either its politics or its design principles and ultimately becoming mildly irritated by its determination to hold the moral high ground. In the early 1890s, for example, Blomfield was an active member of the Art Workers' Guild and a partner along with W. R. Lethaby, Ernest Gimson, and Sidney Barnsley, in the short-lived furniture-making firm of Kenton & Co. However, by 1897 he was propounding the heresy that "an architect is not bound to show every detail of his construction, however ugly it may be. The ultimate justification of architecture is that it should be stable and

RIGHT The house as machine: Le Corbusier's Villa Savoye at Poissy (1929–31). "Reinforced concrete ought to do a lot for us," Shaw once said to Lethaby. Le Corbusier and a whole future generation of architects proved his prediction right.

beautiful." Nine years later, when it was suggested that architectural students at London's Royal Academy ought to be given lectures on arts and crafts subjects, Blomfield responded by saying: "I have come to the conclusion that the Arts and Crafts Movement has done more harm than good to Architects."

While the neo-Georgians were dismissing good, honest construction and quiet vernacular in Britain, the Arts and Crafts movement in continental Europe was marginalized by trends that made its own reforms seem tame. False ornament, which disguised an object's true nature, was wrong, said Ruskinian orthodoxy. No, all ornament was wrong, said Modernists including Adolf Loos: "the evolution of culture marches with the elimination of ornament from useful objects." A hard new functionalist aesthetic was appearing, one that admitted the realities of the industrial age, embraced the future, and sought to create an entirely new design vocabulary. "The artist posseses the ability to breathe soul into the lifeless product of the machine," declared Walter Gropius; and such steel and glass wonders as his Fagus Factory at Alfeld an der Leine (1911), or Le Corbusier's use of reinforced concrete frames for domestic housing, gave the lie to Ruskin's belief that "modern industrial construction methods were eternally separated from all good and great things." ("Reinforced concrete ought to do a lot for us," Shaw had told Lethaby in 1900.)

Hindsight though, should not blind us to the real legacies of the Arts and Crafts movement: the liberation from overstuffed Victorian vulgarity; the discovery — for that is almost what it amounts to — of good design and the total work of art; the joy in simple vernacular buildings; the realization that architecture and the decorative arts are underpinned by a moral imperative. And, of course, there is its greatest achievement, in which those rather highflown and abstract notions join together and become real — the Arts and Crafts house itself.

LEFT **Embracing industrialization: the Fagus Factory at Alfeld an der Leine, by Walter Gropius and Adolf Meyer (1911). By the 1910s, the Modern movement's eager acceptance of new construction methods left the Arts and Crafts movement looking like a quaint Victorian anachronism.**

BIBLIOGRAPHY

Aslet, Clive: *The Last Country Houses* (Yale University Press, 1982)

Backemeyer, Sylvia, and Gronberg, Theresa, eds: *W. R. Lethaby, 1857–1931: Architecture, Design and Education* (Lund Humphries, 1984)

Barron, P. A.: *The House Desirable* (Methuen, 1929)

Battersby, Martin: *The World of Art Nouveau* (Arlington Books, 1968)

Bosley, Edward R.: *The Gamble House* (Phaidon, 1992)

Boutelle, Sarah Holmes: *Julia Morgan: Architect* (Abbeville, 1995)

Brown, Jane: *Gardens of a Golden Afternoon* (Allen Lane, 1982)

Crawford, Alan: *C. R. Ashbee and the Guild of Handicraft* (Cheltenham Art Gallery and Museum, 1981)

Crosland, T. W. H.: *The Country Life* (Greening, 1906)

Cumming, Elizabeth, and Kaplan, Wendy: *The Arts and Crafts Movement* (Thames and Hudson, 1991)

Davey, Peter: *Arts and Crafts Architecture* (Phaidon, 1995)

Dernie, David, and Carew-Cox, Alastair: *Victor Horta* (Academy, 1995)

Dixon, R., and Muthesius, S.: *Victorian Architecture* (Thames and Hudson, 1985)

Duchscherer, Paul, and Keister, Douglas: *The Bungalow: America's Arts and Crafts Home* (Penguin Studio, 1995)

Eaton, Leon: *Two Chicago Architects and Their Clients: Frank Lloyd Wright and Howard Van Doren Shaw* (MIT Press, 1969)

Faulkner, Peter, ed.: *Arts and Crafts Essays by Members of the Arts and Crafts Exhibition Society* (Thoemmes Press, 1996)

Fellows, Richard A.: *Sir Reginald Blomfield* (Zwemmer, 1985)

Garnham, Trevor: *Melsetter House* (Phaidon, 1993)

Gifford, John: *The Buildings of Scotland – Edinburgh* (Penguin, 1984)

Girouard, Mark: *Sweetness and Light: The Queen Anne Movement 1860–1900* (Yale University Press, 1984)

Girouard, Mark: *The Victorian Country House* (Yale University Press, 1979)

Gow, Ian: *The Scottish Interior* (Edinburgh University Press, 1992)

Greensted, Mary: *Gimson and the Barnsleys* (Alan Sutton, 1980)

Hall, Michael: *The English Country House* (Mitchell Beazley, 1994)

Harvey, Charles E.: *William Morris: Design and Enterprise in Victorian Britain* (Manchester University Press, 1991)

Hausen, M.; Mikkola, K.; Amberg, A.; and Valto, T.: *Eliel Saarinen: Projects 1896–1923* (Otava, Helsinki, 1990)

Hewitt, Mark Alan: *The Architect & the American Country House 1890–1940* (Yale University Press, 1990)

"Hilles," *Country Life*, lxxxviii, 212, 234

Hitchmough, Wendy: *C. F. A. Voysey* (Phaidon, 1995)

Hoffmann, Donald: *Frank Lloyd Wright's Hollyhock House* (Dover, 1992)

Hollamby, Edward: *Red House* (Phaidon, 1991)

"Home Place", *Country Life*, xxvi, 634

Howkins, Alun: *Reshaping Rural England – A Social History 1850–1925* (HarperCollins, 1991)

Hussey, Christopher: *The Life of Sir Edwin Lutyens* (Country Life, 1950)

Hussey, Chrstopher: *The Work of Sir Robert Lorimer* (Country Life, 1931)

Jackson, Frank: *Sir Raymond Unwin* (Zwemmer, 1985)

Jekyll, Gertrude: *Colour Schemes for the Flower Garden* (Country Life, 1936)

Kelmscott Manor: *An Illustrated Guide* (Society of Antiquaries of London, 1996)

King, Anthony D.: *The Bungalow: the Production of a Global Culture* (Routledge & Kegan Paul, 1984)

Kornwolf, James D.: *M. H. Baillie Scott and the Arts and Crafts Movement* (Johns Hopkins Press, 1972)

Lambourne, Lionel: *Utopian Craftsmen* (Astragal, 1980)

Latham, Ian: *Joseph Maria Olbrich* (Academy Editions, 1980)

Lethaby, W. R.: *Philip Webb and his Works* (Oxford University Press, 1935)

Maas, Henry; Duncan, J. L.; and Good, W. G., eds: *The Letters of Aubrey Beardsley* (Cassell, 1970)

Macaulay, James: *Hill House* (Phaidon, 1994)

MacCarthy, Fiona: *William Morris* (Faber and Faber, 1994)

MacCarthy, Fiona: *All Things Bright and Beautiful: Design in Britain 1830 to Today* (George Allen & Unwin, 1972)

"Melsetter House," *Country Life*, clxx, 566

Moffat, A.: *Remembering Charles Rennie Mackintosh* (Colin Baxter Photography, 1989)

Morris & Co.: A Brief Sketch of the Morris Movement, and of the Firm Founded by William Morris (Morris & Company, 1911)

Muthesius, Hermann: *The English House* (BSP Professional, 1987)

Ottewill, David: *The Edwardian Garden* (Yale University Press, 1989)

O'Gorman, James F.: *Living Architecture: a Biography of H. H. Richardson* (Simon & Schuster, 1997)

O'Neill, Daniel: *Sir Edwin Lutyens: Country Houses* (Lund Humphries, 1980)

Parry, Linda: *Textiles of the Arts and Crafts Movement* (Thames and Hudson, 1988)

Pevsner, Nikolaus: *Pioneers of Modern Design* (Penguin, 1984)

Pevsner, Nikolaus, et al: *The Buildings of England* (Allen Lane, 1951 onwards)

"Ragdale, The Country Home of Mr Howard Shaw," *Architectural Review*, January 1904, 23–26, 108

Rubens, G.: *William Richard Lethaby: His Life and Work* (Architectural Press, 1986)

Ruskin, John: *The Seven Lamps of Architecture* (G. Allen, 1894)

Ruskin, John: *The Stones of Venice* (Allen & Unwin, 2 vols, 1904)

Saint, Andrew: *Richard Norman Shaw* (Yale University Press, 1976)

Sembach, Klaus-Jurgen: *Henry van de Velde* (Thames and Hudson, 1989)

Society for the Protection of Ancient Buildings, Annual Reports (1878–1902)

Stansky, Peter: *Redesigning the World: William Morris, the 1880s, and the Arts and Crafts* (Princeton University Press, 1985)

Steele, James: *Barnsdall House* (Phaidon, 1992)

Stickley, Gustav, et al: *Stickley Craftsman Furniture Catalogs* (Dover, 1979)

Storrer, William Allin: *The Architecture of Frank Lloyd Wright* (MIT Press, 1974)

Strong, Roy: *Country Life 1897–1997: The English Arcadia* (Country Life, 1996)

Tinniswood, Adrian: *Historic Houses of the National Trust* (National Trust, 1991)

Tinniswood, A.: *Life in the English Country Cottage* (Weidenfeld & Nicolson, 1995)

Van Rensselaer, Mariana G.: *Henry Hobson Richardson and His Works* (Dover, 1969)

Voysey, C. F. A.: *Individuality* (Chapman and Hall, 1915)

Weaver, Lawrence: *Small Country Houses of Today* (Country Life, 1910)

Weaver, Lawrence: *Houses and Gardens by E. L. Lutyens* (Country Life, 1913)

Whiffen, Marcus: *American Architecture Since 1780* (MIT Press, 1969)

Woodbridge, Sally B.: *Bernard Maybeck, Visionary Architect* (Abbeville, 1992)

INDEX

Page numbers in *italic type* refer to picture captions.

A

Adcote, Shropshire *50*
adobe 92–5
Aesthetic Movement 18, 53
Ahler-Hestermann, Friedrich 151
Albro, Maxine *101*
All Saints, Selsey 19
Allingham, Helen 114
Alma-Tadema, Lawrence 25
Anderson, R. Rowland 159, 161
Anthony, Earle C. 75–6
architecture 40–1
    mail-order 80, 86, 87, *87*
    vernacular 27, *30*, 31, 35, *35*, 37,
    41, 66, 75, 92–3, 111, 119,
    136, 161, 169
Ardkinglas, Argyll 159
Armstrong, William 22–3
Arroyo Craftsman 86
Art and Craft of Garden Making
    (Mawson) 117
Art Nouveau 43, *45*, 55, *55*, *142*,
    151, 154–7, *154*, *155*, *156*
Art-Workers' Guild 35, 100, 118,
    123, 130, 134, 148, 159, 166
Arthurian legends 14, 34
Arts and Crafts Architecture (Davey)
    124
Arts and Crafts Exhibition Society
    6, 35, 42, 61, 148–9, 159, 166
Ashbee, C. R. 25, 52, 72, 73, 135,
    143, 149
Atelier Elvira, Munich *154*, 155
Athenaeum, The 24
Austria 53, *143*, *149*, 155, *155*

B

Baillie Scott, M. H. 52, 57, 58,
    80, 106, 107, *115*, 117, 153
Baldwin, Fred 137
Barn, The, Exmouth 130
Barnsdall, Aline 88–90
Barnsley, Ernest 40, 41, *61*, 66,
    107, 123, 134, 135, 142, 166
    Rodmarton Manor 136–9, *136*,

137, *139*, 142
    Upper Dorval House 61, *61*
Barnsley, Sidney 40, *41*, 69, *107*,
    123, 134, 135, 139, 142, 166
Barton St Mary, Sussex 48
Bathurst, Lord 66
Bauhaus 143
Beale, James 30–2, *31*
Beale, Margaret 30–1, *32*
Beardsley, Aubrey 151, 154,
    155–6
Bedford Park, London 52, 126–9,
    126, *128*
Behrens, Peter 42, 52, 53, 55
Belgium 155, *156*
    Bloemenwerf 40, 41, 42–5, *42*,
    43, *45*
    Les Vingt 42, 149
Benson, W. A. S. 21, 25, 29, 32
Berry, B. F. *126*
Bess-Scott, William *13*
Biddle, Arthur *148*
Biddulph, Claude and Margaret
    136–7, *136*, 139
Bilson, James 123
Bing, Samuel 154
Blackie, Walter W. 150–3, *151*
Bloemenwerf, Uccle 40, 41, 42–5,
    42, *43*, *45*
Blomfield, Reginald 123, 166, 169
Blow, Detmar 25, 41, *63*, 69, 123,
    132, 142
    Hilles 41, 62–5, *62*, *65*
Bodley, G.F. 19, 159
Boroughby, Cambridgeshire *25*
Bosselt, Rudolf 52, 55
Bournville, Birmingham *128*, 129
Brewer, Cecil 135
Bridges, Robert 25
Briggs, Arthur Currer 118–20,
    118
Broadleys, Windemere 118–21,
    118, *119*, *120*
Brown, Ford Madox 19, 29
Buckley, J.W. 120
Bucknell, Alfred 66, *123*
Bucknell, Norman *123*
Builder, The 57, 137, 148

Bulletin of Arts & Crafts, The 86
Bungalow Magazine, The 86–7
Bürck, Paul 52, 55
Burden, Bessie 17, 20
Burden, Jane *see* Morris, Jane
Burford, Oxfordshire 24
Burne-Jones, Edward 6, *9*, *16*, 17,
    19, 20, *21*, 25, 29, 34, *51*, 148,
    149
Butterfield, William 16
Byrdcliffe Colony 72
Byrne, Arthur 94, *94*

C

Cadbury family *128*, 129
California 72–3, 86–7
    Casa del Herrero 92–5, *92*, *93*,
    94
    First Church of Christ Scientist
    74
    Gamble House 73, 82–5, *82*,
    84
    Gillette Ranch 96–9, *97*, *98*
    Grayoaks *73*, 74–7, *74*, *75*, *76*
    Hollyhock House 88–91, *88*,
    89, *90*, *91*, 162, 165
    Williams House 100–3, *100*,
    101, *103*
    see also Los Angeles
Campfield, Mrs 20
Carlisle, George Howard, 9th Earl
    31
Carlyle, Thomas 25
carpets 18, 21, 29
Carr, Jonathan T. 128
Casa del Herrero, Montecito
    92–5, *92*, *93*, *94*
Central School of Arts and Crafts,
    London 35
ceramics 21
Chaplin, Charlie 98
Chaucer, Geoffrey 17
Chermayeff, Serge 143
Chicago 72, *72*
    Coonley house 48
    Glessner House 144–7, *144*,
    146, *147*
    Oak Park *72*, 162

Ragdale 41, 46–9, *47*, *48*, *49*
Chipping Campden,
    Gloucestershire 52
Christ Church Cathedral, Oxford,
    Vyner Memorial window *21*
Christiansen, Hans 52, 55
Coe & Robinson 128
Colinton Cottage, Edinburgh 161
Collinson & Lock 32
Colour Schemes for the Flower Garden
    (Jekyll) 115
communities, artistic 87
    Byrdcliffe Colony 72
    Guild of Handicrafts 52
    Hvitträsk 56–9
    Matildenhöhe 52–5
    Roycroft 72
    Sapperton 40, 61, 66, 69, *69*
communities, model 128–9,
    128, *129*
concrete 162, *162*, 165, *165*, *166*,
    169
Coonley house, Chicago 48
Cotswold Group 40, *41*, 61, 66,
    69, *69*, *107*, 122, 123, *123*,
    124, 130, 134, 135, 136, 139,
    139, 142, 166
Cottage Homes of England (Dick) 114
Country Life 41, 60, 65, 68, 87,
    108–9, *108*, *109*, *132*
country life, idealization 60–1,
    106–7, 114, 126
Country Life in America 87, 98
Country Life building, London 109
Coxen, Budleigh Salterton 123
Craft Revival 136, 139, *139*
Craftsman, The 73, 78–81, 83, 86
Craftsman Farms, Morris Plains
    87
Craftsman Workshops 78–81, *78*,
    79, *80*, *81*, 83, 93
Cragside, Northumberland 22–3,
    22, *23*
Crane, Walter 6, 21, 25, 42, *51*,
    72, 128, 148, *148*, 149, 154
Crooksbury, Surrey 48, 111
Crystal Palace 6, *6*
Curwen 20

D

Daneway 66
Das englische Haus (Muthesius) 50–1
Davey, Peter 124
Davidson, William 151
De La Warr Pavilion, Bexhill-on-
    Sea 143
de Morgan, William 6, 21, 25, 29,
    128, 146
Deanery Garden, Sonning 109
Dearle, J.H. 21, 29, 32
Defence of Guinevere, The (Morris) 14
Deutscher Werkbund 143
Dick, Stewart 114
Dietrich, E. G. W. 79
Domestic Revival 58, 133, 162
dress reform 43, *43*

E

Earlshall, Fife 159, 161
Eklund, Jarl 58–9
Ellis, Harvey 80
embroidery 17, 18–19, 20, 21, 32,
    32, 79
Endell, August *154*, 155
England 6–9
    Bedford Park 126–9, *126*, *128*
    Broadleys 118–21, *118*, *119*,
        120
    Cotswold Group *see* Cotswald
        Group
    country life, idealization 60–1,
        106–7, 126
    Cragside 22–3, *22*, *23*
    Das englische Haus (Muthesius)
        50–1
    garden city movement 129
    Hilles 41, 62–5, *62*, *65*
    Home Place 117, 130–3, *130*,
        132, *133*
    model communities 128–9,
        128, *129*
    Morris & Co. *see* Morris & Co.
    Munstead Wood 48, *106*,
        110–13, *110*, *111*, *112*, *114*
    New Earswick 129, *129*
    Owlpen Manor 41, *41*, 66–9,
        66, *67*, *68*, *69*
    Port Sunlight 129
    Red House 14–17, *14*, *16*, *17*,
        22, 31, 32, 60
    Rodmarton Manor 136–9, *136*,
        137, *139*, 142
    Ruskin *see* Ruskin, John
    Society for the Protection of
        Ancient Buildings 24–5, 62

Standen 30–3, *30*, *31*, *32*
    Stoneywell Cottage 62, 122–5,
        122, *124*
    Upmeads *60*, 61
    Upper Dorval House 61, *61*
    Wightwick Manor 26–9, *26*,
        29, *32*, 116–17
English Flower Garden, The (Robinson)
    114
Ennis House, Los Angeles 162
Ernst Ludwig Haus, Matildenhöhe
    53, 55
Exeter Guildhall, Devon 25
exhibitions 148–9
    1851, Great Exhibition, London
        6, *6*, 9
    1862, International Exhibition,
        London 19, 148
    1876, Centennial Exhibition,
        Philadelphia 148, *148*
    1883, Foreign Fair, Boston 72,
        144, 148
    1888, Arts and Crafts
        Exhibition Society, London 6,
        148
    1893, World's Columbian
        Exposition, Chicago 83
    1896, Arts and Crafts
        Exhibition Society, London 159
    1900, Vienna Secession 149,
        151
    1900, World's Fair, Paris 53, 56,
        57
    1901, *Ein Dokument deutscher Kunst*
        53, 55
    1902, Turin International
        Exhibition of Modern
        Decorative Art 151
    1906, Arts and Crafts
        Exhibition Society, London 166
    1915, San Francisco Exposition
        74

F

Fagus Factory, Alfeld an der Leine
    169, *169*
Fairbanks, Douglas 98
Fallingwater, Pennsylvania 162
Faulkner, Charles 14, 17, 19, 20
Feure, Georges de 155
Finland
    Hvittorp 56–7
    Hvitträsk 41, *41*, 56–9, *56*, *57*,
        58, *59*
First Church of Christ Scientist,
    Berkeley 74

fitness for purpose 12
Formakin, Renfrewshire 159
Foster, Myles Birket 114
Four, The 150–1
Frampton, Kenneth 162
France 154, 155, *155*, *166*
Frost, Robert 80
furniture 17, 51, 72
    Craftsman Workshops 78–81,
        78, *79*, *80*, *81*, *83*, 93
    Gimson and the Barnsleys *41*,
        69, *69*, 107, 123, *123*, *124*,
        130, 134, 135, 139, *139*, 142,
        166
    machine production 81, 134–5
    Morris & Co. 19, 20, *20*, 21,
        32, 37
    van de Velde 40, 43, *43*

G

Gallé 154, 156
Gamble House, Pasadena 73,
    82–5, *82*, *84*
garden city movement 129
Gardening magazine 114
gardens 30, *47*, 51, *106*, *111*,
    114–17, *115*, *116*, *117*
Gaudí, Antoni 155, *156*
Gaye, Howard *119*, 120
Georgian Revival 32, 166, 169
Germany 51, 143, 155
    Fagus Factory 169, *169*
    Haus Olbrich 41, 52–5, *52*, *53*,
        55
Gesellius, Herman, Hvitträsk (with
    Lindgren and Saarinen) 41, *41*,
    56–9, *56*, *57*, *58*, *59*
Gill, Irving 80, 93
Gillette, King Camp 96–8, *96*
Gillette Ranch, Calabasas 96–9,
    97, *98*
Gimson, Ernest 25, 40, 61, 66,
    69, *69*, 107, 123, 130, 134,
    135, 142, 143, 166
    Stoneywell Cottage 62, 122–5,
        122, *124*
Gimson, Margaret 123
Gimson, Mentor 123
Gimson, Sydney 123
Glasgow Group 150–1, 159
Glasgow School of Art 151
glass 20, 29, 154, 155, 156
    see also stained glass
Glessner, John J. and Frances 144,
    146–7
Glessner House, Chicago 144–7,

144, *146*, *147*
GLS 56–9
Godwin, E.W. 128, 148, *148*
Goldman, Emma 88
Gothic Revival 12, 22, 75, 126,
    143, 155
graphics 43
Grayoaks, Marin County *73*,
    74–7, *74*, *75*, *76*
Greene, Charles Sumner and
    Henry Mather 9, *83*
    Gamble House 73, 82–5, *82*,
        84
Griggs, F.L. 68, 69
Gropius, Walter 142
    Fagus Factory 169, *169*
Guild of Handicrafts 52, *143*
Guimard, Hector 155, *155*, 156
Gummerus-Ehrström, Olga 59

H

Habich, Ludwig 52
Hacienda del Pozo de Verona,
    Pleasanton 93
Haddon Hall, Derbyshire 27
Hall, John and Peter 83
Hardy, Thomas 25
Haus Olbrich, Matildenhöhe 41,
    52–5, *52*, *53*, *55*
Hazlitt, William 107
Heal, Ambrose 134–5, *134*
Heal, John Harris 135
Heal & Son 21, 32, 134–5, *134*,
    135
Hearst, Phoebe 93
Hearst, William Randolph *94*, 101
Heinemann, Arthur S. 86
Hesse, Ernst Ludwig, Grand Duke
    52, 55
Hill House, Helensburgh *142*,
    150–3, *150*, *152*, *153*, 161
Hilles, Gloucestershire 41, 62–5,
    62, 65
Hillside Club, Berkeley 86
Hoffman, Josef *143*, 149
Hollyhock House, Los Angeles
    88–91, *88*, *89*, *90*, *91*, 162,
    165
Holme, Charles 41
Home Place, Norfolk 117, 130–3,
    130, *132*, *133*
Homestead, The, Frinton-on-Sea 61
Homewood, Hertfordshire 48
Honeyman and Keppie 150–1
Hoover, J. Edgar 88
Hopps, J.H. 74–5

Horta, Victor 155, *156*
Hôtel Autrique, Brussels 155
Hôtel Tassel, Brussels 155
House Beautiful 87
Houses and Gardens (Baillie Scott) 106
Hubbard, Elbert 72
Huber, Patriz 52, 55
Hudson, Edward 108–9, *109*
Hunt, William Holman 25, 29, 34
Hurst, The, Sutton Coldfield 35
Hussey, Christopher 65
Hvittorp, Helsinki 56–7
Hvitträsk, Helsinki 41, *41*, 56–9, *56, 57, 58, 59*

I
Ibberson, Herbert 66
Ideal House, The 41
Iford Manor, Wiltshire *116*
Impressionism 42
Industrial Revolution 9, 12, 34, 134
Ionides, Alexander 31
Italy 155

J
Jack, George *20*, 21, 25, 31, 32
Japanese influence 83–4, *83, 148*
Jeffrey & Co. 20
Jekyll, Gertrude *47*, 109, 114–16, *114*
    Munstead Wood *106*, 110–13, *111*
Jenney, William Le Baron 47
Jesmond Dene, Northumberland 23
Jewell, S. & J. 32
jewellery 19, 20, 21, 155
Jewson, Norman 41, *61*, 66–9, *66*, 137, 142
John, Augustus *63*
Jones, Inigo 40
Jugend 155
Jugendstil 155

K
Keats, John 107
Keeler, Charles 75, 86
Kelmscott Press 72, 149
Kelsmcott Manor, Oxfordshire *9*, 66, 106, *108*
Kemp, Edward 114
Kempe, Charles Eamer 27, 29, *29*
Kenton & Co. 123, 166
knit-block construction 162, *162*, *165*, *165*

L
Ladies' Ecclesiastical Embroidery Society 101
Ladies' Home Journal 72, 87
Lalique, René 155
Lamont house, Lake Forest, Chicago 48
Laverockdale, Edinburgh 158–61, *158, 159, 161*
Le Corbusier 42, 142, 169
    Villa Savoye *166*
Letchworth, Hertfordshire 129
Lethaby, William Richard *23*, 25, 31, 48, 51, 61, 101, 109, 123, 156, 166
    Melsetter House 34–7, *34, 35, 36, 37*, 117, 161
Lever, W. H. 129
Liberty 21, 155
light fittings *29, 32, 84, 143*, 153, *153*
Lindgren, Armas, Hvitträsk (with Gesellius and Saarinen) 41, *41*, 56–9, *56, 57, 58, 59*
Lindisfarne Castle 109
Little Moreton Hall, Cheshire 27
Lloyd, Rev. Percy 130–3
London
    1 Holland Park Road 31
    1 Palace Green 31, *51*
    8 Red Lion Square 17, 19–20
    26 Queen Square 20, 83
    Bedford Park 52, 126–9, *126, 128*
    Central School of Arts and Crafts 35
    Country Life building 109
    Great Exhibition 6, *6*, 9
    Merton Abbey *18, 19*, 20
    St James's Palace 18
    South Kensington Museum, Green Dining Room 18
Long Copse, Surrey 61
Loos, Adolph 42, 169
    American Bar, Vienna *149*
Lorimer, Sir Robert Stodart, Laverockdale 158–61, *158, 159, 161*
Los Angeles
    Hollyhock House 88–91, *88, 89, 90, 91, 162, 165*
    Luther Dodge House 93
    Storer House 162–5, *162, 165*
    see also California
Loudon, J. C. 114
Lowell, Amy 80

Lubbock, Sir John 25
Luther Dodge House, Los Angeles 93
Lutyens, Edwin 48, 51, 109, *111*, 116, *116*, 132, 142, 166
    Munstead Wood 48, *106*, 110–13, *110, 111, 112*
Lympne Castle, Kent 159

M
Macartney, Mervyn 123
MacDonald, Frances 150–1
MacDonald, Margaret 149, 150–1
Macdonald, Ramsay 139
machine production 81, 134–5
Mackail, J. W. 16
Mackenzie, R. W. 159
Mackintosh, Charles Rennie 51, 149, 155, 159
    Hill House *142*, 150–3, *150, 152, 153*, 161
MacNair, Herbert 150
Mahler, Gustav *58*
mail order *73*, 80, *80*, 86, 87, *87*
Maison and Atelier Horta, Brussels 155, *156*
Maison de l'Art Nouveau 154
Mander, Flora 26–9, *117*
Mander, Samuel Theodore 26–9, *27*
Mander, Sir Geoffrey and Lady 29
Mangle, Harry 110, *111*
Maple's 32
Marshall, Peter Paul 19
Marx, Harpo 98
Matildenhöhe community, Darmstadt 52–5
Matthews, Charles 35
Mawson, Thomas 117
Maybeck, Bernard 74–6, *74*, 86, 101
    Grayoaks *73*, 74–7, *74, 75, 76*
Mayer, Adolf, Fagus Factory 169, *169*
Melsetter House, Orkney 34–7, *34, 35, 36, 37*, 117, 161
Mendelsohn, Erich 143
Merton Abbey, London *18, 19*, 20
metalwork 17, 20, 21, *29, 32, 43*, 66, 72
Meyrick-Jones, Rev. F. M. 133
Middlemore, Theodosia 34–5, 37, *37*
Middlemore, Thomas 34–5, 37
Millard Residence, Pasadena 162
Mission Revival 93, 100

Modern British Domestic Architecture and Decoration (Holme) 41
Modern Movement 42, 53, *60*, 61, 142–3, *149*, 169, *169*
Modern Painters (Ruskin) 29
Modernisme 155
Mooney, Tom 88
Moorcrag, Cumbria 49
Moorcrag, Windemere 120
Morgan, Julia 101
    Williams House 100–3, *100, 101, 103*
Morris, Jane *9*, 14, 17, 20
Morris, Marshall, Faulkner & Co. 13, 17, 18–20, 148
Morris, May *9*, 17, 21, 35, 37, 151
Morris, Talwin 151
Morris, William *6, 9*, 12–17, *12*, 43, 51, 62, 66, 73, 86, 101, 106, 108, *108*, 123, 126, 130, 134, 142, 148, 149, 159, 166
    carpets 18, 29
    furniture *9*, 17, *20*, 21
    Society for the Protection of Ancient Buildings 24–5
    wallpaper and textiles 17, 20, *20, 27, 32*, *32*, 79
Morris & Co. 12–21, *18, 19, 20, 21*, 26, 27, 29, 31–2, 35, 37, 63, 72, 135, 146, 148, 149
Mount-Temple, Lady 13
Mucha, Alphonse 155
Munstead Wood, Surrey 48, *106*, 110–13, *110, 111, 112, 114*
murals 16, 17, 19, *101*
Muthesius, Hermann 29, 45, 50–1, *50*, 118, 119, *120*, 151, 153, 158–9

N
Nash, John 40
Nashdom, Buckinghamshire 116
National Romanticism 57, *57*
Neff, Wallace, Gillette Ranch 96–9, *97, 98*
Nesfield, William Eden 22, 29, 129
Neue Palais, Darmstadt 52
New Earswick, York 129, *129*
New York 72, 78, *86, 87*
News from Nowhere (Morris) 43, 101, 135, 166
Nicholson, Sir William *31*

O

Oak Park, Chicago 72, 162
Ockwells Manor, Buckinghamshire 27
Olbrich, Joseph Maria 53
    Ernst Ludwig Haus 53, 55
    Haus Olbrich 41, 52–5, 52, 53, 55
    Vienna Seccession Building 53
Old English 22–3, 112, 120, 128, 128, 129
Old Pound House, Wimbledon 60
Orchard, The, Chorleywood 41, 49, 119
Ould, Edward 26–9
Owlpen Manor, Gloucestershire 41, 41, 66–9, 66, 67, 68, 69
Oxford 14, 19

P

Painter, William 97
Paris 154, 155
Parker, Barry 129
Patmore, Coventry 25
Paxton, Joseph, Crystal Palace 6, 6
Payne, Henry 132
Petersfield, Hampshire 24
Peto, Harold 116
Pevsner, Nikolaus 130, 142–3, 156
Philistine, The 86
Pissarro, Camille 154
plasterwork 23, 29, 37
Plumpton Place, Sussex 109
Port Sunlight, Cheshire 129
Powell, Alfred 61, 139
Powell, Louise 139
Powell & Son 20
Pre-Raphaelite Brotherhood 29
Prinsep, Val 31
Prior, Edward Schroeder, Home Place 117, 130–3, 130, 132, 133
Pugin, Augustus Welby 12, 75, 143

Q

Queen Anne Revival 52, 74, 126, 128

R

Radical Romanticism 76
Ragdale, Lake Forest, Chicago 41, 46–9, 47, 48, 49
Red House, Bexleyheath 14–17, 14, 16, 17, 22, 31, 32, 60

Ricardo, Halsey 63
Richardson, Henry Hobson 144
    Glessner House 144–7, 144, 146, 147
Richardsonian Romanesque 144
Riddell, George 108
Robinson, William 114
Rodin, Auguste 154
Rodmarton Manor, Gloucestershire 136–9, 136, 137, 139, 142
Romanticism 107
Roosevelt, Theodore 97
Rossetti, Dante Gabriel 13, 13, 14, 17, 19, 29, 66
    stained glass 19
Rothenstein, John 139
Rothenstein, William 66, 139
Rowntree, Joseph 129, 129
Roycroft community 72
Ruskin, John 12–13, 13, 14, 25, 26, 29, 43, 51, 62, 72, 73, 79, 86, 103, 126, 129, 134, 142, 143, 149, 169
Ruskin Club, Berkeley 86
Russell, Gordon 143
Ryerson, Edward L. 48

S

Saarinen, Eero 57
Saarinen, Eliel 57
    Hvitträsk (with Gesellius and Lindgren) 41, 41, 56–9, 56, 57, 58, 59
Sagrada Familia, Barcelona 155, 156
St Andrew's, Roker 130, 132
St Giles's Cathedral, Edinburgh 159
St Michael's, Brighton 19
Salutation, Kent 116
Samuel Freeman House, Los Angeles 162
Sandburg, Carl 80
Schindler, Rudolph M. 88, 90
Schweinfurth, A. C. 93
Scotland
    Hill House 142, 150–3, 150, 152, 153, 161
    Laverockdale 158–61, 158, 159, 161
    Melsetter House 34–7, 34, 35, 36, 37, 117, 161
Scott, George Gilbert 24, 75
Scottish National War Memorial, Edinburgh 159

Scrubey, William 139
Sedding, John Dando 66, 123
Seurat, Georges 42
Shaw, Howard Van Doren 47
    Ragdale 41, 46–9, 47, 48, 49
Shaw, Richard Norman 29, 35, 51, 66, 112, 123, 129, 130, 142, 166, 169
    Adcote 50
    Bedford Park 128
    Cragside 22–3, 22, 23
Shepley, Rutan & Coolidge 144
Sherman, General William T. 92
Silver, Joel 165
Simpson, G. B. 30
Small Country Houses of Today (Weaver) 60–1, 122–3
Smith, George Washington, Casa del Herrero 92–5, 92, 93, 94
Smithers, Leonard 156
Snowshill Manor, Gloucestershire 115, 117
socialism 35, 65, 139, 166
Society for the Protection of Ancient Buildings (SPAB) 24–5, 62
Spain 155
Spanish Colonial Revival 93, 98
Speed, Harold 118
stained glass 18, 19, 21, 27, 29, 58, 72, 84, 132
Standen, Sussex 30–3, 30, 31, 32
Stanway, Gloucestershire 63
Stapley, Mildred 94, 94
Steedman, George F. 93–4
Stephen, Leslie 25
Stevens, Ralph 92
Stickley, Gustav 73, 78–81, 78, 83, 86, 93
    Craftsman Farms 87
Stickley, Leopold and George 81, 81
Stile Liberty 155
Stones of Venice, The (Ruskin) 12, 26, 43, 135
Stoneywell Cottage, Ulverscroft 62, 122–5, 122, 124
Storer, Dr John 165
Storer House, Los Angeles 162–5, 162, 165
Street, G. E. 14, 16, 24, 66
Strong, Sir Roy 109
Studio, The 55, 57, 119, 134, 156, 166
Suburban Villa and Garden Companion (Loudon) 114

Sullivan, Louis 144
Sussex chair 20, 21
Sweet, Edward E. 86
Swinburne, Algernon 17
Symbolists 42

T

tableware 17
Talmadge, Thomas 46
tapestries 43, 63
Tatler, The 41
Taylor, Tom 107
Terry, Ellen 128
Tewkesbury Abbey, Gloucestershire 24
textiles 18–19, 18, 19, 20–1, 27, 32, 63, 132
Tiffany 154
tiles 17, 20, 128
timber-framed buildings 26, 27
Tintinhull House, Somerset 116
Tipping, H. Avray 109
Tomes, Sir John 31
Trinity Church, Boston 144, 146
typography 43

U

United Crafts 78
United States 72–3, 86–7, 148
    Casa del Herrero 92–5, 92, 93, 94
    Craftsman Workshops 78–81, 78, 79, 80, 81, 83, 93
    First Church of Christ Scientist 74
    Gamble House 73, 82–5, 82, 84
    Gillette Ranch 96–9, 97, 98
    Glessner House 144–7, 144, 146, 147
    Grayoaks 73, 74–7, 74, 75, 76
    Hollyhock House 88–91, 88, 89, 90, 91, 162, 165
    Oak Park 72
    Ragdale 41, 46–9, 47, 48, 49
    Storer House 162–5, 162, 165
    Williams House 100–3, 100, 101, 103
    Willitts House 143
Unwin, Raymond 129
Upmeads, Staffordshire 60, 61
Upper Dorval House, Sapperton 41, 61, 61
Upwood Gorse, Caterham 31
urbanization 126–9

V

Valance, Aymer 119
van de Velde, Henry *40*, 43, *43*,
     51, 154
   Bloemenwerf *40*, 41, 42–5, *42*,
     43, *45*
Van Gogh, Vincent 42
Van Nu en Struks 43
Van Rensselaer, Mariana Griswold
     146, 147
Vanbrugh, Sir John 40
Vidor, King 98
Vienna *155*
   American Bar *149*
   Secession 149, 151, 155
   Secession Building 53
Villa Savoye, Poissy *166*
Vingt, Les 42, 149
Voysey, Charles Francis Annesley
     48, 49, 57, 80, 118–19, *118*,
     135, 142, 151, 153, 156, 166
   Broadleys 118–21, *118*, *119*, *120*

The Homestead 61
The Orchard 41, 49, *119*

W

Waals, Peter 139
Wade, Charles Paged 117
Wagner, Otto *155*
wallpaper 20–1, *20*, 27, 31–2, 43,
     146
Wardle, George 72, 148
Watts, G. F. 25
Weaver, Lawrence 60–1, *108*, 109,
     122–3, 124, 130
Webb, Philip *14*, 19–21, 25, 35,
     62, 66, 101, 142, 143, 156,
     162
   furniture 16–17, 19, 32
   Red House 14–17, *14*, *16*, *17*,
     22, 31, 32, 60
   Standen 30–3, *30*, *31*, *32*
Weimar School of Applied Arts
     45

Wells, H. G. 166
Wells, Randall 132
Westerlund, Robert Emil 56
Whistler, James Abbott McNeill
     18, 53
White House, Helensburgh 153
Whitehead, Ralph Radcliffe 72
Wiener Werkstätte *143*
Wightwick Manor,
     Wolverhampton 26–9, *26*, *29*,
     32, 116–17
Wilde, Oscar 18, 26, 29, 53, 151,
     155–6
Williams, Selden 103
Williams House, Berkeley 100–3,
     100, *101*, *103*
Willitts House, Illinois *143*
Windyhill, Kilmacolm 151
Witley School 114
Wood, Edgar *60*, 61
Wordsworth, William 107
Wren, Sir Christopher 40

Wrenaissance 23, 60, 83, 109,
     112, 116, 166
Wright, Alfred 137, 139
Wright, Eric Lloyd 165
Wright, Frank Lloyd 46, 80, 87,
     89, 144
   Fallingwater 162
   Hollyhock House 88–91, *88*,
     89, *90*, *91*, 162, 165
   Oak Park *72*, 162
   Prairie houses 89, 162
   Storer House 162–5, *162*, *165*
   Taliesin 89
   Willitts House *143*
Wright, Lloyd *88*, 165

Y

Yeats, W. B. 148
Yellow Book 155
Young, Basil 123

ACKNOWLEDGMENTS

PUBLISHER'S ACKNOWLEDGMENTS
The Publishers would like to thank Tracey Beresford, Penny Warren, and Clare Peel for their invaluable contribution to this project.

PICTURE ACKNOWLEDGMENTS
The Publishers would like to thank especially the following people for their help with the picture research: Martin Charles; Camilla Costello and Olive Waller of The Country Life Picture Library; Eric and Liz Thorburn of The Glasgow Picture Library; and Mary Greensted of the Cheltenham Art Gallery & Museum.

KEY TO ABBREVIATIONS
AAM Archives d'Architecture Moderne; **AFK** A. F. Kersting; **AJ** Augustus John ©The Estate of Augustus John 1999, All rights reserved, DACS; **AKG** AKG, London; **AL** Andrew Lawson; **APA** Axiom Photographic Agency; **ARC** Arcaid; **ARS** ©ARS, NY and DACS, London 1999; **AS** Arthur Sanderson & Sons; **AVE** Andreas von Einsiedel; **AVSS** Alexander Vertikoff/Originally published in *American Bungalow Style* (Simon & Schuster); **BAL** Bridgeman Art Library; **BFM** Bildarchiv Foto Marburg; **BS** Bruce Smith; **CAGM** Cheltenham Art Gallery & Museum, Gloucestershire; **CAL** Special Collections, California Polytechnic State University; **CB** Corbis-Bettman; **CCS** Crown Copyright: Royal Commission on the Ancient and Historical Monuments of Scotland; **CED** College of Environmental Design/Bernard R. Maybeck Collection (1956–I); **CFC** Craftsman Furniture Catalogues; **CI** Christie's Images; **CL** Chiswick Library; **CLPL** The Country Life Picture Library; **DB** Dover Bookshop; **EBDW** reproduced by permission of Elizabeth Banks/Derrick E. Witty; **EL** Erich Lessing; **EPWA** Esto Photographics/Wayne Andrews; **ET** Eric Thorburn; **ETA** E. T. Archive; **FAM** Finland Arkitektur Museum; **FLG** F. L. Griggs; **FLW** Courtesy of The Frank Lloyd Wright Archives, Scottsdale, AZ.; **GH** The Gamble House; USC; **GHM** The Glessner House Museum, Courtesy of the Glessner House Museum Chicago, IL.; **GPL** The Glasgow Picture Library; **HGPL** Hulton Getty Picture Collection; **HI** Hilbech; **HLD** Hessisches Landesmuseum Darmstadt; **HLH** Department of Printing and Graphic Arts, The Houghton Library, Harvard University; **JD** J. Dessauler; **JG** Jonathan Gibson; **JGL** John Glover; **JM** Jane Martindale; **JMO** James Morris; **JRF** Joseph Rowntree Foundation; **LL** Lucinda Lambton; **MC** Mike Caldwell; **MCH** Martin Charles; **MF** Mark Fiennes; **MFR** Michael Freeman; **MJ** Martin Jones; **NB** Nic Barlow; **NCS** Neil Campbell-Sharpe; **NM** Nicholas Mander; **NME** Nick Meers; **NPG** National Portrait Gallery; **NT** Natalie Tepper; **NTPL** National Trust Photographic Library; **NTS** Courtesy of The National Trust for Scotland; **NTSPL** National Trust for Scotland Photo Library; **OPG** Octopus Publishing Group Ltd; **PC** Private collection; **PH** Phillips Auctioneers; **PR** Paul Rocheleau; **PRA** Paul Raftery; **RB** Richard Bryant; **RC** Richard Cheek; **RF** Ragdale Foundation; **RIBA** Royal Institute of British Architects; **RT** Rupert Truman; **SB** Simon Biddulph; **SD** S. Desow; **SOT** Sotheby's Picture Library; **SPAB** Society for the Protection of Ancient Buildings; **V&A** Victoria and Albert Museum; **VHHM** Courtesy of Victor Horta House Museum, Brussels; **VMFA** Virginia Museum of Fine Arts, Richmond. Gift of Sydney and Frances Lewis/Katherine Wetzel; **WDG** William Doyle Galleries, NY; **WI** Wissenschaftsstadt; **WMG** William Morris Gallery; **WMMC** Wightwick Manor, The Mander Collection /Derrick E. Witty; **WPL** Woodmansterne Picture Library.

Front Cover AS (UK), MCH (US); **Back cover** GPL/ET; **Endpapers** NTPL/AVE ; **1** NTPL/NME; **2** PR; **6** HUL; **7** ETA/V&A; **8** WMG; **9t** ETA, **9b** AFK; **10** APA/JMO ; **12** CB; **13** HUL; **14** NPG; **15** GPL/ET; **16** MCH; **17** GPL; **18cb** WMG; **19tcr** WMG; **20r** AS, **20bcl** BAL; **21r** WPL; **22** NTPL/RT; **23** NTPL/AVE; **24cb** SPAB; **25cr** SPAB, **25bcl** SPAB; **26–27b** NTPL/RT; **27l** NTPL/WMMC ; **28** ARC/RB/1987; **29** NTPL/AVE, **29bcl** MCH; **30** NTPL/RT; **31l** NTPL/RT, **31r** NTPL/EBDW; **32** NTPL/MC; **33** NTPL/MC; **34** MCH; **35** MCH; **36** CLPL/JG ; **37** CCS; **38–39** PR/ARS; **40** AAM; **41t** ARC/RB, **41b** JM; **42b** AAM/JD; **43tl** AAM, **43br** VMFA; **44** AAM/SD; **45br** AAM/SD; **46tcr** RF, **46b** EPWA; **47** RF; **48** RF; **49br** RF; **50tc** OPG; **51tl** AKG, **51bl** OPG; **52** HLD; **53tl** HLD, **53tr** WI; **54** HLD; **55br** HLD; **56b** FAM; **57tl** FAM, **57br** ARC/RB; **58** ARC/RB; **59t** FAM; **60** CLPL; **61t** CLPL, **61b** CAGM; **62** CLPL; **63** PC/AJ; **64** CLPL; **65** CLPL; **66t** NM, **66b** JM; **67r** NM; **68t** CAGM /FLG; **69br** JM; **70–71** MFR/ARS; **72** PR; **73t** BS, **73b** AVSS; **74t** CED ; **74b** BS; **75** BS; **76–77** BS; **78t** DB /CFC; **78b** CI; **79** WDG; **80** DB; **81** CI; **82** MFR; **83** GH; **84tr** GH, **84bl** ARC/RB; **85** ARC/RB/1992; **86** AVSS; **87** AVSS; **88–89b** ARC/NT/ARS; **89t** FLW; **89b** ARC/NT/ARS; **90l** MFR/ARS; **90–91** MFR/ARS; **92** RC; **93** RC; **94** RC; **94–95** RC; **95** RC; **96bl** CB; **98–99** ARC/MF; **100** BS; **101t** CAL; **101b** BS; **102** BS; **103t** BS; **104–105** ARC/LL; **106** JGL; **107** BAL/CAGM, **107b** CAGM; **108** CLPL; **109t** CLPL; **109tl** CLPL, **109cb** CLPL, **109b** PC; **110t** ARC/RB; **111tl** CB, **111b** JGL; **112–113** CLPL; **114bl** CLPL; **114–115** NTPL/NME; **116tcl** NTPL/NCS; **116 bcr** CLPL; **117** JGL; **118** MCH, **118b** NPG; **119t** RIBA; **119b** MCH; **120** MCH; **121** MCH; **122** CLPL; **123tl** BAL/CAGM, **123bl** BAL/CAGM; **124–125** CLPL; **126–127** CL; **128tl** ARC/MF, **128br** CL; **129** JRF; **130–131** CLPL; **132bl** CLPL; **133t** CLPL; **134tcr** OPG, **134bl** PH ; **135bl** PH; **136tc** SB, **136tr** SB, **136bl** MCH; **137b** SB/AL; **138–139** CLPL; **140–141** MFR/ARS; **142** MCH/NTS; **143t** PR, **143b** SOT; **144** HLH; **145** PR/GHM ; **146** PR/GHM; **147** PR/GHM; **148t** AKG, **148b** SOT; **149** AKG/EL; **150** GPL; **151** NTSPL; **152–153** GPL; **153** MCH/NTS; **154** BFM; **155t** ARC/NB, **155b** CI; **156tr** ARC/RB/ ©DACS 1999, **156bl** ARC/PRA; **157** ARC/VHHM/RB/© DACS 1999; **158** CCS; **159tl** CCS, **159br** CLPL; **160–161** CLPL; **162–163** ARC/RB/ARS; **164** MFR/ARS; **165** ARC/RB/ARS; **167** ARC/MJ ©FLC/ADAGP, Paris and DACS, London 1999; **168–169** AKG/HI